EMBRACE THE
CHAOS

EMBRACE THE
CHAOS

BE THE MASTER OF CHAOS

MY STORY

BY

KURT GASSNER

My-mindguide.com

Embrace the Chaos
Kurt Gassner

Impressum
My-mindguide – The publishing trademarke of trendguide Capital GmbH, Klenzestr. 42a, 80469 Munich, Germany.

Reg. Nr. HRB Munich 206639, VAT 152 123 159, CEO: Kurt Friedrich Gassner
Web: www.my-mindguide.com, mail: gassner@my-mindguide.com

Paperback ISBN: 978-3-949978-36-4
Ebook ISBN: 978-3-949978-38-8
Hardback ISBN: 978-3-949978-38-8

TABLE OF CONTENTS

Rethinking yourself -
AUTHOR'S NOTE -

Dear reader,

I am delighted that you're reading this book, primarily because it was born out of years of ups and downs. As you flip through these pages, you'll understand that chaos is a part of our life and also you will discover how I dealt personally with chaos, disruptions and changes. As an practical example I will share my own story from my humble beginning. I am fully aware that my story is not an exceptional one and therefore you will read also about other people who crossed the sea and mastered the storms

If you've picked this book off the shelf—whether literally or metaphorically—you probably felt the need to because, maybe, more than just for knowledge, there's this sense of familiarity you have with the subject matter: chaos.

The majority of us, at some point in our lives, have had it rough and tough. We've been at crossroads. Maybe you're currently at one. I have longed to write this book for years now, and I did so to let you know that no matter how freezing cold the winter gets, summer will come, and the sun will shine bright again. That being said, the bitter truth is that all the chaotic change is part of the process. Even though you have that picture-perfect dream or plan for the future, storms can happen, but there's hardly anything you can do to change that. Change happens, and more often than not, it happens without your permission. I intend to make you see that many times, there's no gain without pain and no shortcut to success. In fact, success never even marks the end of your struggle. You have to be prepared—that's the most practical and realistic way to being an overcomer.

I really do hope that after reading this book, you learn so much, put it all into action, and start to see life in a different and realistic way. I also hope my story speaks more than words to you.

Thank you.

Cycle of Life

Death

Birth

Existance

Part One

INTRO TO CHANGE

They say that change is the only constant thing in life. So, if that's a widely accepted concept and if we believe it to be true, then why do we complicate and dread over its manifestation? While that might sound like a rhetorical question, it likely got you thinking or even unconsciously forming an answer. But here's what I think: Just because something is normal doesn't always mean it's pleasant. Just because it's what everyone else has deemed valid doesn't mean it's taken lightly. For instance, death can be considered an equalizer in the sense that it is the ultimate form of change. Truth be told, death is one of the most certain—and last—occurrences in a person's life.

BIRTH ➡ Existence ➡ DEATH

So, if death is the ultimate truth, then why do we mourn the dead? Should the truth not hurt us just because it's inevitable? Of course not. The truth can hurt. Just because something is true doesn't automatically mean we have to be okay with it.

However, we must also consider those who do not believe that the death of the material body is the end of the road. Also I hold onto the notion that the material body is simply changing its form of energy, rather than passing on. In this sense, physical death is not the end; it's simply a milestone on our way as eternal souls.

That being said, the birth of a child often incites joy, happiness, and excitement. But then the child dies—either early or at old age—and a gloomy atmosphere lingers. This is because we don't always think it's a fair trade, even though it's inevitable that a child's life will come to an end. Many people find question the purpose of our coming to life in the first place, especially if in the end, we'll be physically nonexistent. Very often these same people struggle to make sense out of the whole cycle of life and to discover a higher sense. Some end up accepting it as a bitter fact while others fight to accept it at all.

Essentially, people mourn their dead not because they do not accept that death is the ultimate truth, but rather they mourn because it hurts, they think it's unfair, and because the memories, history, and sentiments developed over a period of time have likely created some level of attachment to this individual. And attachment, whenever involved, can make things harder to accept, thus making the things that are truth seem questionable and unfair. It can make us question our prior acceptance of death because we're hurt, pained, and feel sorry for ourselves and for the person that we've lost; we feel it's wrong and cruel. While death is often an abrupt change to adapt to, it's not always accepted as just, even though it might be considered natural.

Change is often accepted theoretically rather than tangibly or realistically. For instance, I acknowledge that change happens, whether abruptly or not, and it's normal; it's a part of life. But just as I mentioned, acceptance in theory doesn't mean we've come to terms with it in reality. In this context, we're talking about unpleasant and abrupt change, as it's the type we often struggle to accept.

Let's consider an example in which a student is accustomed to being at the top of his class. This is how it's been for as long as this student has been in school, and it's likely going to be the case until his graduation. But then, in his senior year, only months away from graduation, a transfer student arrives. It seems like a big change for the new kid, but she climbs the ladder in no time and becomes at the top of her class. The student who was originally at the top of his class didn't anticipate this change—not because he thought change was impossible but because he understood change from a theoretical perspective only. He's shocked that the new girl swiftly and effortlessly rose to becoming number one in the class, moving the star student down to second. It was a change no one saw coming.

For the incumbent, it might be a good thing as things are going pretty well for her around there, but for the other, it's most likely an unpleasant change. He likely felt and processed this abrupt change as awful—a nightmare. If he's an ambitious kid, one whose had everything planned out for himself, then he probably didn't take this change lightly. Though second is great and doesn't determine where a person will be later in life, the fact that he's dropped in status alarms him, and a sense of weakness looms. Even though, in this case, the kid knows that change is the only constant thing in life, it still doesn't make it an easy pill to swallow.

It's one thing to know, say, or think something is true but it's another to accept it and make peace with it. Truth be told, it's only natural to react or feel bad when we find ourselves in unfavorable events that disrupt the serenity, bliss, or stability in our lives. It's never a good experience to suddenly find yourself feeling low when you've been up. It usually requires a whole lot of work to solve or tackle what we perceive as a threat. Drawing on the scenario from earlier, it would be wrong for the boy to solve the problem of being second by cheating on the next test to ensure his grade is higher than the new girl or plotting to sabotage her at school. This would be a negative response to coping or altering the change in his favor. Turning things around, if he, instead of doing what we mentioned earlier, comes to agree that although being number one in the class felt good, it wasn't his birthright or a title that he was the sole holder of. If he honestly comes to terms with the fact that his position in class doesn't define him, then he lets himself understand that he'll be fine as long as he accepts the change. So, instead of reacting negatively or defensively, he does along with the change and works even to be the best again or to quit the race and to discover other personal qualities.

Going with the latter, it would mean that he had not only accepted the change in theory, but also in reality. He chooses to spin what seemed to be a bad into something motivational. Instead of sulking, he decides to grow through the pain and be the bigger person by admitting his hurt and resolving that change can be unpleasant. In the end, he can either learn from it, tactfully make something out of it, or try to fight it and become the villain.

Change can penetrate any realm, including our
1) personal realms,
2) professional realms, and
3) societal realms.

UNDERSTANDING THE DIFFERENT TYPES OF CHAOTIC CHANGE

Personal Change

Life is constantly changing, and presents us with changes that are both positive and negative. Personal changes, such as a breakup, family problems, or health issues, can have a significant impact on our lives and can be incredibly difficult to navigate.

A breakup can be one of the most difficult personal changes that a person experiences. It usually comes with feelings of rejection, loneliness, and sadness—sometimes even nudging us into depression. The ending of a relationship can also lead to a sense of identity loss and a feeling of being physically lost as you navigate this journey called life. The process of healing and moving on from a breakup can certainly take time, which makes it increasingly important to allow yourself to grieve and seek support from friends, family, and loved ones.

A breakup can lead you to find a more compatible partner you otherwise wouldn't have sought out.

Sure, a breakup can be a difficult experience, but it can also be an opportunity for growth and self-discovery. The individual can learn from the mistakes that riddled their past relationship and use it as an opportunity to explore their own needs and wants in a new partner. They can also learn to love and appreciate themselves more, which would improve their future relationships overall. This is only effective, however, if you are adamant about breaking the patterns which initially led you into the first relationship. Breaking this pattern means you have to analyze and reinvent yourself. **Unfortunately**, too many of us get caught in a cycle where we are following our same patterns yet wondering why we aren't getting different results.

Family problems can also cause us stress and turmoil when we are faced with change. Conflicts within a family or between family members can have multiple sources and roots, such as financial problems, communication issues, or differences in values. These conflicts—and at times, confrontations—can lead to feelings of anger, frustration, and helplessness. Should after reading this book these issues are not resolved you should ask for help. It can be a professional therapist but often a close friend can support and help you discover a different perspective and to maintain healthy boundaries within the family.

Family problems can lead to a greater comprehension of the dynamics that exist within a family and can help individuals develop better communication skills. It can also lead to an increased sense of appreciation for the importance of family and the need for healthy boundaries, even with close family members and loved ones, for which many of us tend to believe boundaries are not needed.

Alternatively, if these problems cannot be addressed, then it is also good to practice letting go of all that is not in your control, and all that does not align with the values you've set for yourself.

On that note, experiencing any sort of **health issues** or changes in one's health status can also be a significant personal change that can have a huge impact on our lives. Chronic health conditions, such as heart disease or cancer, often require major lifestyle changes and ongoing management, usually revolving around food, medications, treatment schedules, and exercise. And with these illnesses often comes feelings of frustration, hopelessness, and depression. During these trying times, it is crucial to seek support from healthcare professionals and educate yourself about the condition you have been diagnosed with, as this will allow you to also advocate for yourself and take control of a changing and chaotic situation that is otherwise out of your hands.

In the case of health issues, individuals can learn to better manage their condition and make lifestyle changes that can improve their overall health, and possibly help the mitigate the effects of their new diagnoses. Told in a shortcut: accept the diagnoses but not the prognosis. It's up to you to create even a medical miracle.

They can also develop a greater appreciation for their own health and the importance of self-care. It is important to note that most health issues are caused by a lifestyle that doesn't support our needs; therefore, it's crucial to understand and discover what your body truly needs, and to listen to it in hopes of improving your overall health.

In all these cases, self-care, both physically and emotionally, is crucial to help us overcome the hurdles that change presents us with. This can include as exercise, meditation, or therapy. It can also involve seeking support from friends, family, or a support group.

It is also crucial to remember that personal changes are simply part of life, and that they can ultimately lead to growth and development, as well as identity formation.

Professional Change

Professional changes can come in many forms, and one of the most common is facing a lay off or a company downsizing. There's a possibility of this occurring when a company is facing financial difficulties, not staying within budgets, or when a specific division or department needs to be restructured to better align with the company's changing vision or mission. When a person is laid off, it's not uncommon for them to experience stress that is then translated to other areas of their life. They may feel a sense of loss, insecurity, and uncertainty about their future.

Let's say a company undergoes a merger, and the employees of the acquired company are laid off as part of the restructuring process. These employees may have been with the company for a long time and have a strong attachment to their job, and the layoff can be a difficult experience for them. They may feel a sense of loss, insecurity, and uncertainty about their future. The employees who are laid off may not have any warning and may have to leave their job without any notice.

Another type of professional change that people can experience is a demotion. This happens when an employee is moved from a higher-level position to a lower-level one within the same organization. Poor performance, organizational restructuring, or changes in the company's business strategy can be causes of demotion. A demotion can be an arduous experience for employees, as it is usually perceived as a setback in the individual's career and can lead to feelings of failure, frustration, and embarrassment, especially since the individual demoted usually remains within the same company and department. For example, a sales manager is demoted to a sales representative due to poor performance. The demotion can be a difficult experience for the sales manager, as it can be seen as a setback in their career, and may even mean they are now working under someone who once worked under them, which many may find demeaning.

A career change is another type of professional change that many of us will or have experienced before. This occurs when an employee decides to leave their current job to pursue a new career or field. This can be challenging because it requires employees to start from scratch in a field and may require additional training or education, and may even require a significant increase in effort to keep up with others who have been in the field for years. It can also be a difficult experience for employees who have been in the same field for a long time, as they may feel a sense of loss and uncertainty about their future.

In sum, professional changes can come in many forms and can have a significant impact on employees. From experiencing a job loss to downsizing, demotion, and career changes, it's not uncommon to feel feelings of uncertainty, fear, and turmoil as the future before you begins to blur. However, it is important for employees to be prepared for these types of changes and to have a plan in place for how to navigate them if and when they occur.

Societal Change

There is a vast variety of societal changes that can take place, all of which have a significant impact on our lives. One of the most significant changes that has recently occurred is the Covid-19 pandemic, which has affected us all on a global level.

A pandemic can have a wide range of impacts on individuals, communities, and economies. It can lead to widespread illness and death, as well as significant disruptions to daily life, including school closures, travel restrictions, and changes to work and social interactions. The Covid-19 pandemic has also had a major impact on the global economy in recent years, leading to widespread job loss and economic downturns, as well as inflation.

Another type of societal change is war, which has a devastating impact on individuals, communities, and nations alike. It often leads to loss of life and displacement, as well as significant damage to infrastructure and the economy. War can also have long-term impacts on mental and physical health, and can lead to ongoing issues such as poverty and political instability. The ongoing war in Ukraine is a prime example of how war can have a devastating impact on a country, leading to loss of life, displacement of people, and damage to infrastructure and the economy.

Economic changes can also have a significant impact on society. A recession, for example, can lead to widespread job loss and financial insecurity for all. The 2008 financial crisis is a prime example of how a recession can have a significant impact on the global economy. The crisis led to job loss, foreclosures, and economic downturns around the world, and the impacts had a ripple effect that lasted for several years after the crisis had supposedly come to an end.

Moreover, climate change is another societal change that is impacting the world. Climate change is causing extreme weather events, rising sea levels, and changes in temperature and precipitation patterns. These changes can have a significant effect on individuals, communities, and economies, leading to loss of life, displacement, and damage to infrastructure and the economy, as well. Like other changes, it can also impact physical and mental health.

A societal change that is not always considered but has a significant impact on people is a political change. This can include changes in government policies, laws, or leadership that can affect the lives of people in a specific country or region. For example, healthcare system changes or school funding changes can impact the way we live or day-to-day lives, forcing us to adapt to an everchanging society.

Societal changes can come in many forms and can have a significant impact on our lives. Pandemics, war, economic changes, climate change, and political changes are examples of societal changes that can have a wide range of effects on individuals, communities, and economies. It is important for individuals, communities, and nations to be prepared for these types of changes and to have plans in place for how to navigate them. Had we prepared for the Covid-19 pandemic ahead of time, we may have made it out fast and stronger, with minimal damage being inflicted on ourselves, our communities, our healthcare systems, and our government. Additionally, it is important for governments and organizations to provide support and resources for those affected by societal changes.

That being said, change can be a two-way street and I will point out that there is often not that much of an emotional difference. When change happens, it could be: 1) good/positive, or 2) bad/negative.

GOOD/POSITIVE CHANGE

Change does not always have to be cold and harsh. It can, at times, be warm, pleasant, or refreshing. This kind of change is one that's perceived as good or positive. For example, would you consider the transition from state senator to president of the country a positive change? Absolutely! It's a positive change because it's an uplift in status, a win, and a victory. Moreover, what if a stock you had invested in only decreased in value from the day you purchased it, but then, suddenly, it boomed, making you ten times richer than you were? Even though you might have been disappointed or heartbroken initially, you would now consider the sudden change positive. You would feel ecstatic. Again, this is a welcomed change—a positive and favorable one.

In short, good/positive change is accepted because it benefits us. However, even positive change can come with consequences and side effects that ultimately contradict its meaning. This means that changes we consider positive can cause us to experience some trouble.

Positive change can, at times, wreak havoc in our lives—or at least we may feel like it does. The difference between positive and negative change is usually the severity and longevity of these effects—that is, how long we experience those effects. Sometimes, when we experience positive change, it takes us some time to adjust and recognize that such change is, in fact, positive. More than that, positive change also comes with its own set of challenges, particularly in terms of introducing uncertainty, disrupting our routine and habits, putting strain on our relationships, bringing new challenges and responsibilities, and impacting our mental and physical health. It can take us some time to process it, come to terms with it, then move on to accepting and living with it.

One way that positive change can cause stress is by introducing uncertainty into our lives. When things are changing, it can be hard to predict how they'll turn out in the end, which is often anxiety-inducing. For example, getting a promotion at work may be exciting, but it can also bring stress as you adjust to new responsibilities and expectations.

Furthermore, positive change can cause stress by disrupting our established routines and habits. When we are used to doing things a certain way, it can be hard to adjust these set routines and schedules. For example, getting married may bring a lot of positive changes, but it can also disrupt our daily routines and make us feel out of our element. It forces us to adapt our perspectives, routines, communication strategies, and more, so we can merge our lives with another, not to mention merging our lives with our partner's family, friends, and schedule, as well. Although love and happiness will be at the core of this change, the difficulties and obstacles still remain, making it a positive change that can, at times, feel challenging.

On that note, positive change can also put strain on our relationships. When our lives are changing, it can be hard to maintain the same level of connection and intimacy with the people around us. For example, starting a new job or going back to school can take up a lot of our time and energy, leaving us feeling drained when it comes to spending with our friends and family. Although this may not be intentional, we may simply learn to put more effort into our relationships and adapt to other ways of maintaining connections during times in which time does not permit like it may have before.

Additionally, positive change may also bring new challenges and responsibilities, which can be both overwhelming and stressful. For example, becoming a parent can bring a lot of joy and satisfaction, but it can also be a lot of work and responsibility. Caring for a child and learning to navigate your relationship with your partner at the same time given this new added responsibility is not easy; there will be a lot of firsts, a lot of good times, a lot of fights, and a lot of nights spent in worry and anxiety. As you figure out how to balance your role as a parent and as a partner, you'll experience something referred to as *role strain* in the field of sociology, in which the stress an individual feels stems from societal expectations placed on them to simultaneously fulfill multiple roles in their lives (i.e., the roles of a parent and a business owner).[1]

Positive change can also cause stress and strain on our mental and physical health. When we experience a significant amount of stress, it can be hard to take care of ourselves and make healthy choices. For example, if we are feeling overwhelmed by the changes in our lives, we may be more likely to neglect our physical and mental health, in the sense that we may sleep or exercise less, skip meals, or reduce time spent for self-care.

Let me take you through a practical illustration for better comprehension: The birth of a new baby in a family of three. Maria is the first child and she's six years old. This is a major change in Maria's life, almost as much as it is for her parents. Although this change is one that the family anticipated, the actual manifestation of this change could have consequences that are different than those Maria and her parents prepared for. So, when the new baby finally arrived, it took a toll on the family.

I. Although Maria's mom felt relieved and happy about the baby's arrival, she was still processing this new change. Physically, she felt tired, sore, and in pain from the labour and stitches she had received while giving birth. Mentally, she felt exhausted, uncertain, and burdened. She smiled whenever other family members, friends, and acquaintances

---

1 Happy. (2022, November 21). *What is role strain? how it differs from role conflict?* Psychcrumbs. Retrieved January 23, 2023, from https://psychcrumbs.com/what-is-role-strain-in-sociology/#:~:text=Role%20strain%20is%20a%20term,time%20work%2C%20and%20social%20life.

came around to see their "new bundle of joy" and congratulate them. She was happy about it, but her uncertainty and exhaustion about the change and the process of adjusting to it all clouded her positive feelings about the development. Still, she sucked it all in, and on the outside, she appeared to be a joyous and ecstatic new mother of a handsome baby boy.

II. Now, let's move on to Maria's dad. He was also exhausted—almost as much as his wife—as a result of the preparation and alterations he's made so both his wife and new baby would be comfortable. He had to call his mother to help watch Maria while he ran to the hospital to ensure everything went well. He was relieved when the doctor let him know that his baby was delivered safely. He spread the news to his family and friends and was very happy. However, mentally, he was still burdened with worries of making sure everything was perfect. And even though he and his wife had worked out a plan that covered the expenses for their new baby, he still felt overwhelmed by it and the added responsibility of raising two kids.

Both parents remembered how it felt when they had Maria. They remembered the significant change they experienced, the compromises they made, and the responsibilities that came along with all, and this made them both feel sentimental and anxious at the same time. They realized they were facing a new route on their parental journey

III. And now, the little member of the nuclear family, Maria. For Maria, as a child, it might have been fun seeing her mum go through the pregnancy stage with her protruding stomach. That is, she likely recalled the good days, like visiting the park, family outings with just her, Daddy, and Mummy with her growing belly. But what she didn't expect was the actual change that came along with her mum's pregnancy, which, unlike her parents who knew better, seemed to have occurred abruptly. Even though she might not have fully understood the whole pregnancy, labour, and delivery thing, she understood that things were changing right before her very eyes and there was nothing she could do about it. She somehow felt like an outcast in her own family. At the first sight of the baby in her mother's arms with her dad by their side, she felt an ache in her chest of which she couldn't tell was heartbreak. But for what it was worth, she could tell she wasn't feeling as ecstatic as her parents were about the new member. She felt that her perfect little life was crashing because of this new development and her position as her parents' top priority was changing. She sensed the new one was zapping all the affection in the room. So, when her parents signaled to her to come by the bed and meet her baby brother, she froze and just stared on with gloomy eyes. In that moment, she still wasn't convinced that the new baby wasn't a threat to her, that he wasn't there to change her life from awesome to sad. And when she finally met her baby brother, she refused to have anything to do with him. She thought the way he shrunk and stretched was alarming. She never wanted to touch or carry him because he looked fragile, and his shrieking cries made her upset. She felt jealous, sad, and left out. Many times, she felt invisible, unloved, and uncared for by her parents. And sometimes, she wished things had remained the way they used to be: just she and her parents, without no intruder. While everyone managed to take the change as a positive one, she struggled to come to terms with it or recognize the positivity in it.

Her parents will have to do a lot of convincing, soothing, and reassuring to make her see and accept that the new change is fine and didn't mean the life she used to know was going to be altered the way she feels it would. They would recognize her reservations and feelings about the whole new change and would have to fix it. They would tell her how much fun it would be having a younger sibling. They'd paint mental pictures of blissful scenarios of such in her innocent little head and they would reassure her that nobody could make them love her less. They would tell her that the arrival of her baby brother might be overwhelming for her, but it was also overwhelming for them. They'd make her understand that they all had roles to play now, and she was to love and protect her baby brother. They would make her see how good it could be for the two of them; the role of a big sister could be fun. And while they have these moments with Maria, they would not only be setting things straight and better with her, but also with themselves because they, too, in the process, would come to recognize their own feelings and insecurities regarding the new change.

This is only an illustration, which is practical and realistic enough for us to understand that even positive change can have a negative impact on us. Another deeper truth is, these effects, at times, if not correctly dealt with, tackled, or managed, can lead to long term damage. For example, spinning the case study above around, if Maria's parents do not manage the situation well with Maria and instead push her away while focusing on the newborn, the bond between them and their daughter could start thinning out or could gradually cause resentment to build inside her, either against her parents, her baby brother, or both. Alternatively, it could cause Maria to become withdrawn as she deals with feelings of dejection caused by underlying feelings of being unloved, left out, or useless. This would result in a troubled childhood (which could go on to affect her as a teenager or an adult) where she could exhibit negative behavioural patterns, such as disobedience, nagging, or crankiness.

Similarly, we could flip things to consider how rough this change could be on the parents if not managed well. It's ironic that what seems to be a positive change like this could actually stir negative feelings and changes in the lives of those going through it. These negative side effects could be as mild as a change in sleep patterns, or as severe as a chronic mental breakdown. In our sample case, a practical example of the negative toll positive change could take on a person experiencing it is, for instance, Maria's mum ending up with post-birth depression. If her feelings were left unmanaged, they could have overwhelmed her mind, which, in turn, could drive her into post-natal depression. And if this happened, it wouldn't only be hard on the new mother, but it could also affect the rest of the family as they would feel the energy through her. She could exhibit sleeplessness, anxiety, or even alcoholism as she seeks refuge in the distraction it could create for her. Physically, she could start losing weight and looking troubled or sick. She could even become abusive as she tries to express the chaos within her. To cut the worse scenario short, what begins as a positive or good change could end up wreaking havoc, disrupting what used to be their peace, orderliness, or serenity, and threatening or breaking Maria's parents' marriage, or even the whole family.

This case study illuminates the notion that if we fail to address the effects of change—even though it is positive change—we may experience a range of negative consequences. These can include physical, emotional, and psychological symptoms, as well as difficulties in relationships and at work.

One of the most common effects of not addressing change is increased stress and anxiety. When the effects of change are not acknowledged or processed, it can cause feelings of uncertainty, insecurity, and a loss of control. These feelings can lead to physical symptoms such as headaches, muscle tension, and fatigue. Over time, chronic stress can also lead to more serious health problems, such as heart disease and depression.

Furthermore, when we don't accept change, we have difficulty adapting. When a person doesn't take the time to reflect on and understand the changes happening in their life, they may find it difficult to adjust to new roles, responsibilities, or environments, making the change even more difficult than it needs to be. This can lead to feelings of frustration and dissatisfaction and may make it challenging for the individual to function appropriately and productively in their personal and professional lives.

Not addressing change can also lead to difficulties in relationships. When a person is not able to process and adapt to change, they may struggle to communicate their needs and feelings to others, which can lead to misunderstandings and conflicts. This can put a strain on relationships and make it difficult to build and maintain healthy connections with others.

In addition to these effects, not addressing change can also lead to a lack of personal growth and development. Change is a natural part of life, and when we don't take the time to reflect on and learn from it, we miss out on opportunities to grow and develop as individuals. This can lead to a sense of stagnation and dissatisfaction with life.

Lastly, not addressing change can also lead to a lack of self-awareness and self-understanding. When we don't take the time to understand and reflect on the changes happening in our lives, we may struggle to understand our own thoughts, feelings, and behaviors. This can lead to difficulty in making sense of our experiences and can affect decision-making and problem-solving.

It is essential to take the time to reflect on and understand the changes happening in our lives so we can effectively cope with them, grow, and develop as individuals. This can be done through journaling, therapy, or seeking support from friends and family, and practicing self-care.

So, if we were to choose which kind of change we want, the positive or the negative, it's mostly certain the case that we'll go for the positive—at least under normal circumstances for the average person. If both forms of change come with cons, then wouldn't we prefer to face whatever consequences the positive change might throw at us? You'll likely agree that coping with positive change seems easier than coping with negative change and the consequences and side effects that accompany both. In other words, accepting positive change can be easier than making peace with the negative.

BAD/NEGATIVE CHANGE

The storms in life can be the beginning of deeper transformation.

Change means something has been altered, and it usually means we have to compromise as a response. Sometimes, change costs us our comfort and sometimes, it just seems like we have to make a lot of sacrifices to adjust to the new normal. We all want the good change, but how many of us would be okay with the bad?

Negative change can be described as the kind of change that usually carries a bundle of unpleasantness with it. Although negative change seems to oppose positive changes, I would argue that they share certain effects. Negative change, such as losing a job, getting your college scholarship revoked, filing for a divorce, or experiencing the death of a loved one, can be destabilizing. Change, whether good or bad, is never easy because it means something has been taken away, added, or tilted in your usual way of life. Additionally, things that require or force us to make changes in the routines, activities, or ways we function can induce stress or tension. For example, moving from a place you've considered home to a new city might be out of your control. It might feel like the life you've built is crumbling or being taken away from you. Letting go of the attachments and relationships you've made during your time in one place can be overwhelming and may seem like too much is being asked of you. It's a lot to sacrifice and can induce a great degree of stress and tension. You suddenly have to create a future that's not even certain. Such a transformation may seem scary and impossible for you to ever adapt to, but the truth is, it *is* possible

Sure, negative change can have dire consequences on our lives, disrupting our sense of stability and security and leaving us feeling overwhelmed and helpless, but there are ways to overcome this. But first, we must understand that the ways in which negative change can manifest ranges from physical and mental health problems to difficulties in personal and professional relationships. A case study of a person going through a negative change can help illustrate the ways in which these consequences can manifest and the impact that they can have on a person's life, as well as strategies for overcoming these challenges and adapting to the changes.

Let's consider a case study of a person named John. John has been working at a large corporation for the last 10 years and in recent months, he's been laid off as a result of company downsizing. This sudden job loss presents a significant negative change in John's life, as it not only affects his financial stability, but it also impacts his sense of identity and self-worth.

One of the most immediate consequences of this negative change for John is financial stress. Losing his job means he will have to change the way he manages and spends his money, as he now faces the possibility of not being able to pay his bills or support his family. This financial stress can lead to further mental health problems, such as depression, anxiety, and difficulty sleeping.

That being said, negative changes *can* still be overcome. For instance, John can adapt to this change by creating a budget and looking for ways to cut back on expenses, as well as looking for alternative sources of income, like freelancing, consulting, or part-time work. He can also seek advice from a financial advisor to help him navigate this difficult situation.

Another consequence of this negative change is the impact on John's mental health. Losing a job can be a very stressful experience, and it can be difficult for John to process and cope with this loss. In fact, 14 out of 16 studies found that job loss leads to significant declines in mental health.[2] He may experience feelings of sadness, anger, and hopelessness, and may find it increasingly difficult to identify a sense of purpose and direction in his life. These feelings can lead to depression, anxiety, and other mental health issues. To overcome this, John can seek professional help from a therapist or counselor, and practice self-care activities, such as exercise, meditation, and journaling to help manage stress and improve mental well-being. He can also consider joining a support group for people who have experienced job loss, which can provide a sense of community and understanding.

---

2 *Unemployment and mental health.* Institute for Work & Health. (n.d.). Retrieved January 23, 2023, from https://www.iwh.on.ca/summaries/issue-briefing/unemployment-and-mental-health

John's relationship with his family and friends may also be affected by this negative change. He may feel too ashamed or embarrassed about losing his job that he may begin to withdraw from social activities and interactions. He may also experience tension and conflicts with his family, as they may not fully understand the extent of his stress and may not know how to support him, while simultaneously, he may not know how to communicate the type of support he needs. To overcome this, John can try to communicate his feelings with his loved ones and ask for their support and understanding. He can also seek help from a relationship counselor or therapist.

In addition to these consequences, John may also have trouble finding new employment. The job market is competitive, and with the current economic situation, it may be hard for him to find a job that is comparable to the one he lost. This can lead to a loss of self-esteem and a feeling of being stuck in a difficult situation. To overcome this, John can consider taking up new skills and training to improve his chances of finding a new job, as well as networking and reaching out to his professional contacts who may be able to help him navigate the competitive job market he has been thrusted into. He can also consider alternative career options that align with his interests and passions.

Furthermore, losing a job can also mean losing a sense of identity and self-worth. John may have defined himself by his career and his role at the company, and now that that is gone, he may feel lost and unsure of who he is and what he wants to do with his life. This can lead to feelings of worthlessness and a lack of motivation.

John's experiences and battle with change helps us better understand the effects negative changes can have on various aspects of our lives, while also shedding light on the fact that negative changes, no matter what they may be, can be overcome with patience, dedication, and a positive mindset.

Change can be like a thief in the night, sneaking up on us when we least expect it and catching us off guard. One moment, everything is familiar and comfortable, and the next, we're thrown into a whirlwind of uncertainty and confusion. It can be like being caught in a storm without an umbrella, with no choice but to ride out the winds of change and hope for the best. But just like the storm clouds eventually clear, change can lead to growth and new opportunities, if we're brave enough to embrace it.

When we think we have everything figured out or planned, and we've set high hopes on our success, it becomes tough to deal with a result other than success. And this could cause a minor to major change in our lives.

It is common for humans to plan ahead. We design our tomorrows as if we have total control, failing to consider how change can navigate or disrupt those plans. While some people adopt the philosophy of living one day at a time, not expecting anything but taking life as it unfolds for them, others would rather plan their whole life events in advance, envisioning a mental one-way route to their happily ever after. Conversely, there are some people who do not only plan their future but also plan *for* the future. Before I move forward in breaking these things down, I would like to outline the categories of people based on their planning habits and approach to dealing with change and chaos: 1) the idealist, 2) the realist, and 3) the middleman.

THE IDEALIST

People that fall under this category are those who plan their future myopically. As mentioned earlier, these people plan without considering that change—usually a chaotic type that can alter their lives such that their plans end up futile—could happen at any point. They believe that once you have a vision, you can achieve it; however, they fail to accept that change and chaos are inevitable. They usually believe that they hold the mantle of their lives and can control who goes on or around it.

Now, to some extent, we *can* control the things that occur in our lives. For example, we can control what we eat, what we wear, where we go, and what we do. But ironically, we don't always control what goes on around us, and as a result, many of our decisions or actions are influenced by our circumstances and external pressures, those we don't choose or have control over.

For these people, living in denial of this can cause them to be disoriented, destabilized, or lose themselves when change happens, whether mild or severe. Not only did they not expect it, but they didn't plan for it, such that its occurrence threw them off guard. For example, a child born with a silver spoon and into a wealthy and influential family always had everything handed right to him—all smooth and rosy. After high school, he planned his future and decided to attend the prestige Harvard University, get a degree in Medicine, then went on to get a master's and PhD. He concluded that he'd get a job in the best hospital in New York City and practice for a while before moving to California, having his own medical center, getting married, then having two kids. After his retirement, he planned on moving to Hawaii and settling.

This sounds like a workable plan for a kid from a wealthy family, right? Right. Circumstances surrounding him influenced his planning. However, this is only the case until at some point along the way, a change he never considered happens and disrupts his plans. For instance, his plans could be derailed by the death of a parent or both parents, even before he started actualizing his plans. The shock, pain, and hurt he might feel after might be such that would be overwhelming, and his grief might be such that leads to depression. He may even pick up negative habits, such as doing hard drugs, abusing alcohol, and so on. Another aspect of change could be if the family entered bankruptcy, experienced a job loss, or experienced the death of a sole provider. These things could sway around and affect his plans. He might feel disoriented and lost so that he falls out on his plans and takes another turn or path entirely different from his initial plans.

Evidently, several consequences are associated with adopting an idealist mentality. One of the consequences an idealist might face is disappointment and frustration. When things do not go as planned, an idealist may feel let down and upset that their vision has not come to fruition, which may make them question their beliefs and aspirations, leading them down a path they had not anticipated, particularly because failure was never on the table.

Furthermore, lack of flexibility and adaptability are also consequences of this mentality. If an idealist is not open to change and does not consider the possibility of things not going as planned, they may struggle to adapt to new circumstances and unexpected events. This can make them inflexible and less able to navigate the complexities of life, which, as we've discussed, are inevitable.

Additionally, an idealist who plans their future without considering changes might face unrealistic expectations. When they hold on tight to their idealistic plans, it may be hard for them to accept when things don't go as expected. This can lead to an unrealistic view of the world and make it difficult for them to manage their expectations. Their perspective becomes warped insofar as they believe that the world will always turn smoothly—that their life will not consist of speed bumps, road closures, and unexpected obstacles.

Furthermore, an idealist who does not consider changes might also face problems in their relationships. When their plans do not come to fruition, they may become distant, unresponsive, and might struggle to interact with others, which can lead to conflicts and misunderstandings.

Basically, an idealist in this context is one who plans their future without considering or believing change can alter them. They believe they can control their own fate or affect other

Idealist

Middle Man

Realist

people's behavior or actions in their favor, whilst pushing to bring their plans to life. Usually, idealists can portray positive traits like determination, but where they usually fall short is not making plans for change or preparing against the *what ifs* that could spring up later and threaten the success and actualization of such future plans.

THE REALIST

Realists are usually balanced. They, unlike idealists, do not only plan the future, but also make plans for the future. What I mean here is that a realist would not only have the future planned but would also have a backup plan in place in case things don't work out. Basically, they're the proactive ones. As they work towards actualizing their future plans, they consider all that could go wrong. They accept that change is inevitable and as such leave space for unforeseen changes or circumstances while planning the future. Sometimes, realists can be as calculative as weighing the pros and cons in everything they do, like perfectionists. Plenty of them think two-ways insofar as they think of both the positive side and the negative side, choose their path accordingly, and work towards it, keeping in mind the uncertainty of things. For plenty of realists, rationalism is priority.

In fact, a strict realist would plan a road trip with friends, make them submit their next of kin details, have their emergency contacts set on their phones, ensure the fire extinguisher is available and ready, ensure there's at least a spare tire, ensure someone, if not all, have pepper spray, and ensure everything's in place just to prepare for unplanned circumstances that could happen on the trip. Some realists may be perceived to be uptight and can be very particular compared to other realists; the severity in behavior may be slight or strong. Realists can equally be perceived as skeptics based on their two-way approach.

So, in short, realists are those who balance the scale. They plan but consider changes—even those that are chaotic. A realist would say, "I want to go to Harvard, get a degree, then go on to get my master's and PhD. *But who knows, anything can happen.*" This is so that the realist can be prepared for any chaotic change. That being said, realists don't always have the solution or backup plan for when change happens, although they mentally prepare for it. Their coming to terms with and accepting that change is inevitable is an attribute that distinguishes them from their idealist counterparts.

Realists tend to be more adaptable and flexible when dealing with change. They are less likely to have rigid expectations and plans and are more open to new possibilities and opportunities. They tend to be more resilient and able to navigate the complexities of life. However, this doesn't always mean that when a change happens along the way, they don't feel it like the idealist would. Change can throw even realists off guard, cause them pain, stress, or worry. For instance, they may struggle to adapt to rapid changes that may disrupt their current routines and way of life. They may also struggle to let go of familiar and comfortable patterns. Additionally, realists may find it difficult to find meaning and purpose in their life, as they tend to be more focused on practicality and daily routine, rather than on ideals or beliefs.

Moreover, realists may experience challenges related to self-doubt and insecurity when faced with change. They may question their own abilities and decisions and may even be less confident in their ability to navigate new situations and challenges.

That being said, the difference between a realist and idealist is in how they handle the change and snap out of it. For a realist who prepared himself against sudden change that could come with transformation, adapting and learning to live with the chaos can be a bit easier and faster than the idealist who had been in denial or failed to consider and prepare for change.

A case study of how a realist and an idealist would deal with a specific negative change can help illustrate the differences in their approaches and the challenges they may face.

Let's consider a case study of a person named Sally. Sally is a recent college graduate who has just gotten engaged to her long-term partner. However, her partner unexpectedly breaks off the engagement. This sudden change in her personal life presents Sally with a significant negative change she must adapt to and overcome.

If Sally were an idealist, she may react to this change by being highly emotional and devastated, having had a clear vision of her future with her partner and having connected her future plans to her the notion of spending the rest of her life with her partner. She may struggle to accept the change, living in a state of denial, and may believe it is impossible to move on. In fact, she may take this negative experience and allow it to ripple into the other parts of her life, derailing her professional life, her career plans for the future, and her relationships with others. Sally may hold on to the belief that things should have turned out differently and may blame herself or her partner for the change, thus dwelling on the experience rather than altering her perspective to ensure she is able to heal from it.

On the other hand, if Sally were a realist instead, then she might be more accepting of the change and may take a more practical approach to dealing with it. She may acknowledge the disappointment of the situation, and surely, she will feel hurt, sad, and heartbroken, but through that pain, she may find the opportunity for growth and self-discovery. Sally may take some time to process the change and reflect on what went wrong and how to move forward. In fact, she likely would have understood that this was a possibility and may have mulled over her reaction to this should it become a reality. Sally may also be more open to the possibility of new relationships and opportunities in the future. She may be more resilient and able to navigate the complexities of this difficult situation.

With this situation illustration our main points, we can begin to understand that the way in which realists and idealists deal with negative change can differ significantly. Idealists may struggle to accept change and may hold on to unrealistic expectations, while realists may be more accepting of change and take a more practical approach to dealing with it. This can help them to be more flexible, adaptable, and resilient in the face of unexpected events.

But there's also another type of persona we can adopt when faced with negative change.

THE MIDDLEMAN

The middleman, unlike the idealist and realist, makes peace with the fact that we can't always control things. The middleman is a very peculiar one of the three. A middleman would say, "Really, I'll take whatever happens. You can't plan these things, you know. Let's just see how things turn out. Let's see how things go." A typical middleman is one who you would ask, "Hey, what do you plan to do after high school?"

And he would reply or even laugh and answer, "I don't know, man. I don't think I have any plans. I'll just go with however life plays out for me."

We can say idealists are optimists and realists are skeptics. A middleman, on the other hand, can be perceived as nonchalant, indifferent, and not necessarily either of the things an idealist and realist are. Their attitude and approach towards things as significant as planning the future or making plans for the future can make people feel like they are not serious about their lives. Rather than having a specific plan to work with, a middleman would rather not have one at all because they usually believe that plans don't always work out. They believe they can't control things or make the future be what they plan it to be. To a middleman, planning can be dramatic and unrealistic. They also believe that change is inevitable, and things are bound to change, so, why make plans when things will likely change anyway? Is it not better to let things play out by themselves?

For a middleman, change is welcomed. This doesn't mean they're not affected by change, whether positive or chaotic. It just means, like the realist, they accept the existence and power of change. Of all these three categories, middlemen can be said to be the most at peace with change and chaos. It's not that they don't feel the negatives or positives that often accompany these two concepts. Rather, the difference between them is that they are the quickest to accept that it is what it is. They tend to snap out of whatever effect change and chaos causes them, accepting the situation as is and acknowledging that there's nothing they can do. It's out of their control. And so, the middleman decides to pick up the pieces of whatever it may be, make something out of it, and move forward with life.

A typical middleman can be recognized as thoughtless by some in situations where their attitude towards the matter is different from the norm. In fact, a typical middleman can be such that he applies the same attitude towards everything and anything. Sentimental issues, such as loss, can be accepted as typical to the extent that they do not grieve—or at least not in the usual ways known to society. This can make people think of these people as heartless, cold, unshaken, wicked, and so on. Meanwhile, this is not necessarily the case. It isn't that they do not recognize the severity of loss, such as the death of a loved. Middlemen can discern these things; however, their expression of them is influenced or altered by how they work (their view on such things, life, or philosophy). So, they often appear cold to those who don't identify with this category.

Let's consider a practical example to help us illustrate this point further. A 14-year-old girl lost her family and pet in a car accident while she was in boarding school. when the sad news reached her, she goes on with her normal routine at school. Although she seemed shocked and saddened by the news at first, she appeared as though nothing had happened much sooner than people expected of her. She didn't cry, though it was clear that she felt sad about what happened to her family and pet. She continued to eat at the cafeteria, attend classes, and do everything as normally as she used to. Even at the funeral, it was very hard to tell who had just lost her family and pet in a ghastly car accident when her friends, family, and acquaintances seemed more sympathetic and in grief unlike the girl herself. It didn't take long before people began to whisper and talk about how coldhearted and numb the girl was. "Can you believe she looks as though nothing even happened to her?" a person stated. "How can a child be that cold about the death of her whole family? I mean, a pet can be understandable in this situation, but her whole family? I think she's either just emotionless or still in the shock or denial," another commented.

This case demonstrates how misunderstood the girl was. In actuality, the girl was just a middleman. She felt the loss, grief, and hurt of the situation, but she coped with it differently than what was considered normal. To her, she was heartbroken by the death of her family and pet. She loved them and enjoyed the moments she had with them. She didn't expect such chaotic change, but quickly accepted the situation because to her, it was a lost battle. She had no control over it and couldn't bring them back. So, she chose to live with her new normal, even though it was not a pleasant one. She decided to live with their memories, move on with life, and see where it would lead her. She didn't know whether she would end up in a good place or a bad one, but she resolved to simply move forward.

Having shared my three categories of humans based on their approach to planning and dealing with chaos and change, let's move back to a concept we discussed earlier: 1) planning the future, and 2) planning for the future.

Inventing the Future

I. Planning the future is when you outline how and what you envision for the future (whether it's planning out a school year, a study schedule, or planning your whole life out). You make a mental representation of these things. At this stage, it usually just consists of the planner, the plan, and steps to achieve said plan that distinguish a future plan from a dream.

II. While planning for the future is usually the realistic part of making future plans, it's sometimes also where you make a backup plan or consider the odds of your plans. It's where you weigh your pros and consider the cons. It's where you consider the *what ifs* and come to terms with the fact that change could happen sometime along the way.

This is usually the part of making future plans that the idealist doesn't perform. And it's the part that the realist would consider in their process of making future plans.

Part Two

CHAOS & CHANGE: CHAOTIC CHANGE

The main motivation for bringing this book to life is my discovery of how we tend to live in denial of chaos and change. How we want the good and don't want the bad. How we sometimes have a picture-perfect representation of life in our heads and think about a happily ever after. We do this because it's easier to deal with peace, serenity, and bliss, and in this process, we often forget that life isn't a utopia. Things go sour. Bad things happen. Negative things are out of our control. Sure, while you're thinking of the good, you might also want to consider that chaos and change can happen. So, when and if it happens, you might have a chance to deal with it better and strategically.

As humans, we try to control things that happen in our lives and around us. We often try to control the chaos that springs up instead of dealing with it. But change is like a wild, untamed creature, always roaming and prowling just beyond our grasp. It's a force we can never fully control, no matter how hard we try. It can come crashing in like a tidal wave, sweeping us up in its violent currents, or it can sneak up on us like a raccoon in the night, stealing our sense of security and predictability. Change can be scary and unpredictable, but it's also a necessary part of life. It's what helps us grow, evolve, and become the best version of ourselves. It reminds us that we are not in control, but also assures us that that's okay. We can learn to ride the waves of change and find the beauty in the uncertainty.

Chaos and change are twin concepts but not necessarily the same. Although they can be used interchangeably at times, change can come with chaos, hence chaotic change, but this might not always be the case. Also, chaos can stir change and demand that alterations be made in what used to be our normal. That being said, chaos and change don't always work together—at least not always at the same time. Essentially, chaos can sometimes come before change happens and demands alterations. For instance, let's consider a child who was born during war and grew up knowing unrest around him. In this case, we can't say much change happened in his life because he was born in the situation and typically grew up under such circumstances. It's the only life he knew. However, chaos surrounds him. From his birth to his growth, it's one thing he's grown to know about his environment.

NOTE: This illustration is only for comprehensive purposes and doesn't imply that chaos means unrest or war.

Still, using the sample case above, if it later happens that the war finally ends and peace is restored or the boy and his family move abroad to a serene and peaceful place, that would be considered change. In this case, a positive one, which can still come with mild chaos that could arise from the change of environment, a language barrier, acculturation, and so on.

So, it's almost like a scheme. See below.

NOTE: In this context, "≈" means "comes before" while "=" means "comes along with")

$$CHAOS \approx CHANGE$$
$$CHANGE \approx CHAOS$$
$$CHANGE = CHAOS$$
$$CHAOS = CHANGE$$

Much of what has been discussed of change in the previous chapter of this book also applies to chaos. Chaos, like change, is inevitable in life. Apart from chaotic situations that can surface, we—more than we like to admit—struggle more with chaos within.

CATEGORIES OF CHAOS

Note the two categories of chaos: 1) chaos within, and 2) chaos without.

CHAOS WITHIN

Chaos within is a type of chaos that occurs internally. It's a type of chaos we usually fight discretely and often do not want to admit to others or even to ourselves. Sometimes, we feel strong emotions related to chaos—ones that linger and disturb us for long periods. Fear, uncertainty, anxiety, sadness, loneliness, depression, hate, jealousy, pressure, low self-esteem, tension, greed, pain, grief, confusion, and anger are some of the most chaotic emotions we can find ourselves struggling to overcome.

These feelings can wreak havoc within us and could make us hate ourselves as a result. We badly want to control these feelings and work hard to appear as calm and put together as we can. Meanwhile, that's not always the case.

While we try to control the chaotic state of our mind, overtime, due to accumulation and shunning the chaos that should have been acknowledged and addressed, things can get even crazier inside us, thus putting our mental health at risk of deteriorating. And while seeking a solution can be as mild as going in for therapy sessions, it could also get as bad as needing to see a psychiatrist.

Instead of trying to accept feelings of hate, jealousy, anxiety, fear, and so on, we lie and convince ourselves that we do not feel them at all. Some run away from admitting these feelings because they perceive them as a sign of weakness and do not want to be seen as weak—not even to themselves.

Chaos within, or internal chaos, also manifests in the workplace, leaking into other areas of our lives when unaddressed and unresolved.

Internal chaos is a common experience when facing change, and can manifest in many ways, such as feelings of uncertainty, confusion, and resistance. This type of chaos can occur when an individual or organization is faced with a significant change, such as a reorganization, merger, or new leadership. The experience of chaos within be overwhelming and can lead to decreased productivity, morale, and mental and physical health.

One of the reasons why internal chaos can occur is a lack of communication and transparency. When individuals are not properly informed about the changes that are taking place, they can feel uncertain about their role and their future. This can lead to confusion and mistrust, and can make it difficult for individuals to adapt to the change. To prevent this type of internal chaos, it is crucial for leaders to openly and honestly discuss the changes that are taking place, and to try their best to involve employees in the process of change, even if in small ways.

Moreover, internal chaos can occur on a professional level due to the fear of the unknown. Change can be scary and uncertain, and individuals may feel like they have no control over their future. This can lead to feelings of anxiety and resistance to change. To prevent this type of internal chaos, it is important to provide employees with information and resources to help them understand and adapt to the change. It's also important to provide support and resources to help employees cope with the emotional aspects of said change.

Furthermore, chaos within can also occur when there is a lack of buy-in or commitment to the change. If employees don't feel invested in the change because they don't fully understand it or believe in it, they may resist it, or feel like it's being imposed on them. To prevent this type of internal chaos, it is important ensure that they understand the reasons behind the change and how it will benefit them and the organization as a whole, as well as them on an individual level.

Dealing with internal chaos in the face of change requires a proactive approach. One effective strategy is to create a sense of shared purpose and vision. This helps employees understand the "why" behind the change and how it fits into the organization's overall mission and vision for the future. This can help reduce resistance and increase buy-in.

Moreover, leaders can provide employees with the necessary resources and support to adapt to the change. This includes providing paid training sessions and educational workshops, as well as access to resources, such as counseling and coaching, to help employees cope with the emotional aspects of change.

It's also important to foster a culture of open communication and feedback. Employees should feel comfortable sharing their thoughts and concerns about the change, and leaders should be open to hearing and addressing them without judgement. This can help employees feel heard and valued and can improve their engagement and commitment to the change.

Finally, it is important to be patient and compassionate during the process of change. Change is never easy, and it can take time for individuals and organizations to adapt. Leaders should be mindful of this and provide employees with the necessary time and support to adjust to the change.

Experience chaos with is common when facing change. By adopting a proactive approach and addressing the emotional and practical aspects of change, leaders can help employees navigate the change process and emerge stronger and more resilient on the other side.

CHAOS WITHOUT

Chaos without takes place outside in places like our environment, our home, our school, our workplace, and so on. This is the types of chaos that we're made to deal with—one we usually didn't create ourselves. Many times, that's just how life works. It's chaotic and there's likely nothing we can do about it.

Chaos around us can be overwhelming. We often struggle with it, not knowing exactly how to react or deal with it. Sometimes, we try to control the chaos; however, that's not entirely possible. For instance, we can't control how people talk or what they say to us, nor their actions against us. We can't control and make people like us or buy into our idea. Usually, however, we can accept the realization and learn to navigate through chaotic situations that may arise.

Rather than worrying or trying to control things that go on around you, try focusing more on the things you *can* control, like your reaction and approach.

External chaos can have a significant impact on our professional lives. Examples of external chaos include changes in the job market, company downsizing, or economic downturns. These types of changes can be overwhelming and can lead to feelings of uncertainty, fear, and stress, as previously discussed.

One of the most common examples of external chaos is a change in the job market. This can occur due to technological advancements, shifting economic conditions, or changes in consumer demand. These changes can lead to a decrease in job opportunities or an increase in competition for jobs, which can

CHAOS
=
CHANGE

be especially difficult for individuals who are looking for work or trying to advance in their careers. To deal with this type of external chaos, it is important to stay informed about changes in the job market and to be proactive in seeking out new opportunities. This may include networking, updating your skills, and being open to different types of job opportunities. It also important to adopt a mindset in which you view this setback as temporary and a part of your long-term journey.

Company downsizing is also an issue related to external chaos, and can occur when a company is facing financial difficulties or is restructuring its business. When this happens, employees may be laid off or demoted, and it can be a difficult experience for those affected. To deal with this type of external chaos, it is important to have a plan in place for how to handle a job loss or downsizing. This may include having a financial safety net, updating your resume, and seeking out job opportunities. It's also important to take care of your mental and emotional well-being during this time.

Economic downturns are another example of external chaos that can occur outside of our control. This can lead to widespread job loss and financial insecurity for individuals and families. To deal with this type of external chaos, it's important to learn how to rapidly deal with a decrease in income. This may include cutting back on expenses, increasing your savings, and finding ways to increase your income or increase your savings through investments.

Dealing with external chaos in the face of change requires a flexible and adaptable mindset. However, having a positive attitude and a sense of perspective can be helpful in dealing with external chaos. It's important to remember that external changes are out of our control and that it's possible to come out of them even stronger and more resilient.

Internal chaos can be like a storm brewing within, brewing uncertainty, confusion, and resistance. External chaos, on the other hand, is like the tempest who arrives unexpectedly, shaking the core of our lives and throwing everything into turmoil. Together, internal and external chaos can create a whirlwind of uncertainty, leaving us feeling disoriented and struggling to find our footing. But just like a storm, it will pass, and with the right mindset and preparation, we can weather the chaos and come out stronger on the other side.

EFFECTS OF CHAOS AND CHANGE

Usually, the realization of uncertainty itself can cause stress and chaos for us. Chaos and change can come with a heavy weight. They can cause us to be stressed when we have to deal with the chaos.

Anxiety is one of the most common symptoms we experience when faced with change, which stems from something called *uncertainty bias,* in which our brain automatically perceives a major life change as negative, thus influencing our ability to make decisions, and consequently increasing our feelings of both anxiety and depression.[3]

---

3 WebMD. (n.d.). *Dealing with change: How it affects your mental health and what you can do to cope.* WebMD. Retrieved January 23, 2023,

Some common symptoms of anxiety in the face of change include:

- Worrying excessively about the future: People who experience anxiety when facing change may constantly worry about what the future holds and how they will cope with the changes that are taking place.

- Physical symptoms: Anxiety can also manifest in physical symptoms, such as increased heart rate, muscle tension, and fatigue.

- Avoiding change: Some people may avoid change altogether in an attempt to avoid the feelings of anxiety that come with it.

- Difficulty in decision-making: Anxiety can make it difficult for people to make decisions, as they may be paralyzed by the fear of making the wrong choice.

- Negative thoughts: People who experience anxiety when facing change may have negative thoughts and beliefs about themselves, such as feeling inadequate or helpless.

- Difficulty concentrating: Anxiety can also make it difficult for people to focus on tasks and pay attention to what is happening around them.

These symptoms can vary in severity and intensity and can also be accompanied by other psychological conditions like depression. It's important to note that not everyone who

---

from https://www.webmd.com/mental-health/what-to-know-about-how-to-deal-with-change#:~:text=When%20a%20major%20life%20change,will%20benefit%20your%20mental%20health.

experiences change will have anxiety symptoms, and that some people may experience anxiety in different ways than others. Additionally, it's also important to seek help if the symptoms of anxiety are interfering with daily life. A therapist or a mental health professional can help the individual to develop coping mechanisms and techniques to manage the anxiety.

Some additional effects that chaos and change can have on us are as follows:

1. Stress
2. Anger
3. Uncertainty
4. Confusion
5. Sadness
6. Crankiness

Change may come like a gust of wind, but with the right tools, we can turn it into a gentle breeze. A toolbox that consists of resilience, adaptability, and a positive outlook can help us make our way through the uncertainty and pave the way for a better and more promising future. We must tend to our emotional and mental well-being, and with the right tools, we can always overcome change and make it work in our favor.

EMBRACING CHAOS AND CHANGE: HOW TO DEAL WITH THEM

Sometimes, I think of how things could have been if we were all handed a life manual that contains a step-by-step guide on how to deal with or permanently overcome challenges that may come our way. Wouldn't life be much easier this way? Well, since that's not how things work around here, we might as well begin finding ways to cope with the chaos and changes life can throw at us.

To embrace the chaos and become the master, then we must learn that the first step to growing can be tough. Sometimes, when life hits us and we're pained, the only reaction is to grow from the pain.

Below, I discuss how to embrace chaos and change.

1. MINDSET RESET

First, to actually be able to master chaos and cope with change, you need to do a mind reset. Here, you want to change your opinions or philosophy, which may hinder your ability to cope with the chaos and change. For instance, if you are more of a utopian thinker or idealist who believes there's always a win-win where you can have it all, you must expect that chaos and change are out of our control and inevitable. Life is not a utopia and things are not always rosy. As they say, "Life is not a bed of roses." So, you want to be more open-minded.

Also, you must learn to stay positive. Nurture your mind toward positivity so that even during chaos or change, you're able to see the positive side to the situation. When you feed your mind with optimism and self-confidence in your ability to fight and thrive despite the chaos or change that comes your way, forcing you to make alterations, it could help minimize the effect these things can have.

It's important to remember that change, whether good or bad, is a natural part of life and it's important to learn how to adapt to it by re-framing your reality. Instead of seeing change as something negative or something to be feared, try to see it as an opportunity for growth and development. Re-frame your thoughts and try to find the positive aspects of the change. This will help you be more open-minded and adaptable and will make it easier for you to navigate the chaos that comes with change. It's also important to understand that change can be a process, not just a one-time event. It's important to take the time to process the change, reflect on it, and learn from it. This will help you to be more resilient and better equipped to handle future changes. And in this sense, you must learn to adopt a growth mindset that embraces challenges and views them as opportunities for further development.

A growth mindset is a way of thinking that allows us to view ourselves as capable of improvement and capable of thriving, no matter our circumstances. It allows us to be more prepared to view change as a challenge rather than a threat, thus altering our perspective and giving us the opportunity to not just overcome the chaos, but to use it to our advantage.[4]

2. BE PREPARED

I advise that you be prepared. If you're interested and wish to be the master of chaos or change, then you should learn to be proactive, like the realist.

---

4 Staff, N. L. I. (2021, November 16). *Why change is so hard - and how to deal with it.* NeuroLeadership Institute. Retrieved January 23, 2023, from https://neuroleadership.com/your-brain-at-work/growth-mindset-deal-with-change

Even though you might not be prepared in a physical or material sense, being mentally ready for chaos and change can really help when it comes to coping with the change when and if it finally occurs. As we discussed earlier, you should not only plan the future but plan *for* the future.

Even though you can't always predict the chaos or change, you can try to envision possible scenarios of change that could occur along the way. Once you do this, you'll be able to plan ahead of these scenarios. This is a pro tip in coping and mastering chaos and change.

Being prepared to face chaos can actually improve the outcome of the situation, as it can help to minimize the impact of the change and make it easier to navigate. But how can we prepare? What steps can we take to plan ahead and ensure we are in a stable condition when we dive into the chaos that will inevitably come our way? Well, preparing for change can take many forms, such as creating a plan, setting goals, and building a support system.

Having a plan in place can help provide you with a sense of direction and purpose, which can be particularly helpful in times of uncertainty. It can also help minimize the impact of the chaotic change by providing a roadmap for how to navigate the situation. Setting specific and achievable goals can also help give you a sense of direction and purpose, making it easier to move forward.

Moreover, it's verry important to build a support system of some sort. Having a strong support system can help provide emotional and practical support during difficult times. This can include friends, family, or professional help. It can also be helpful to seek out a support group or community of people who have gone through similar experiences, whether in-person or online. This can provide a sense of understanding and camaraderie and can help to minimize the feeling of isolation that can come with change.

Additionally, being prepared for chaos can also involve self-care and self-compassion. Taking the time to take care of yourself—both physically and mentally—can help to minimize the impact of the change. This can include things like exercise, meditation, journaling, and spending time in nature.

All in all, being for chaos involves being flexible and open-minded. Being able to adapt to change and being open to new possibilities can make it easier to face the situation. This may include developing a willingness to try new things, to consider alternative solutions, and to be open to new opportunities that may arise as a result of the change.

3. STAY FOCUSED

Coupled with staying positive, staying focused on what is at hand is a great way to master chaos and change. Don't fall out of line because of the chaos or change happening around you. It's not always easy but trying is key. Stay resilient and positive.

The ability to focus on the task at hand and not get sidetracked by distractions or negative emotions can help us navigate the chaos and uncertainty that comes with change.

For example, let's consider Jake, who is a manager at a company that was just acquired, and therefore undergoing a major restructuring. Jack's department is one of the many that are going to be affected by the changes. Jack's initial reaction was to be overwhelmed and anxious, but he decided to stay focused on the task at hand, which was to ensure his team's job security and to help them navigate the change.

Jack came to terms with the notion that he could not control the situation, but he *could* control his focus. So, he decided to remain calm and not let the uncertainty of the situation consume and control him. He focused on the facts and figures. He communicated with his team. He sought out expert advice. It's not necessarily that he ignored the changes and remained in a state of denial; rather, he simply focused on the positive aspects of the change, like potential growth opportunities, and tried to communicate this with his team.

This focus helped Jack face the changes in an effective manner. He was able to lead his team through the restructuring process, and they were able to secure new roles within the company. His team also reported feeling more secure, and more positive about the changes as a direct result of Jack's leadership and guidance.

Moreover, Jack's focus also helped him take care of himself during this difficult time. He made sure to take breaks, practice self-care, and stay in touch with his support system, allowing him to maintain a positive attitude and stay resilient during the changes.

Staying focused during times of change can be a key factor in helping us adapt to the situation and achieve a positive outcome. In fact, staying focused and positive has, at many chaotic points in my life, helped me cope with the change and made me return even stronger after every setback, which I discuss in further detail throughout this book.

4. ACCEPTING THE CHAOS AND CHANGE

Here, you've worked and changed your utopian mindset and adjusted to agree that chaos and change are inevitable. But as I've mentioned earlier, it's one thing to accept chaos and change in theory, but another to actually accept it in a practical sense. When we resist change, we tend to focus on what we have lost or what we are afraid of losing. This can lead to feelings of stress, anxiety, and depression. On the other hand, when we accept change, we are able to focus on the present moment and on the opportunities that change can bring.

Let's take Sarah as an example of how accepting change can be more effective and beneficial than fighting it. Sarah is a successful business owner who has built her company from the ground up. She has always been in control and has always called the shots. However, her company is now facing new competition, and Sarah realizes that she needs to change her business strategy to stay competitive.

At first, Sarah resists the change and fights it. She argues with her team, denies the need for change, and refuses to consider new ideas. As a result, her team becomes demotivated, her sales start to decline, and her company's reputation takes a hit. Sarah finds herself struggling to keep her business afloat.

However, as the situation deteriorates, Sarah eventually comes to terms with the fact that she needs to accept the change. She starts to listen to her team for the first time and seeks out new ideas and strategies to keep her business alive. She realizes that change can bring new opportunities and that embracing it can lead to growth and development.

As a result, Sarah's business starts to improve. Her team becomes more motivated and engaged, her sales gradually increase, and her company's reputation slowly starts to recover. She also finds herself more open-minded and adaptable, and able to navigate the complexities of the business world.

This demonstrates how accepting change can be more effective and beneficial than fighting it. Sarah's initial resistance to change led to negative consequences for her business, while her eventual acceptance of change led to positive outcomes. It illustrates that when we fight change, we miss the opportunity to grow and evolve, and we can find ourselves stuck in a difficult situation, while accepting change can lead to new opportunities and help us to navigate the complexities of life.

So, when chaos or change arise, take a moment or a break to allow yourself to feel all that might come in that moment, like anger, fear, or an emotional breakdown. Once you feel some level of calmness (though reaching here can take time depending on the severity of chaos or change and depending on the individual), work your mind through accepting the chaos and change. The good and the bad. After you've successfully done this, you can then go on to making peace with the realization that you do not control what happens to you or others in life, and chaos and change are inevitable. Accept the situation even though it might not be okay with.

Accept that it is what it is, and that chaos and change are all part of the process. Normal and sudden changes in our lives can and do happen. Make peace and embrace this chaos rather than fighting it.

5. LEARN AND GROW

Chaos and change can be overwhelming for us at times. In fact, at times, it might even seem impossible to get over the effects and adapt to the transformation; however, it is definitely possible.

To learn and grow from chaos and change, we must have accepted, made peace, and embraced the chaos and change. Afterward, we can go on to find a silver lining in the situation. For instance, we can choose to count our blessings instead of focusing on the negatives. We can navigate through the chaos and search for lessons. Instead of sulking and wallowing in negative thoughts or feeling sorry for ourselves, we can accept the chaos, decide to find out where we went wrong, and work through it. We do this all while remaining positive that we'll do it better next time.

Let's take the example of Alex. Alex had always been a city person, working in finance and enjoying the fast-paced life of the city. However, an unexpected job transfer brought him to a small rural town. At first, Alex was resistant to this change, feeling out of place and longing for the city life. But as time went on, he began to explore the town and its surroundings, and discovered a passion for nature and outdoor activities. He started to hike and bike on the weekends, and even found a local gardening group that ran community events and raised money for important environmental causes. Through these new activities, he found a sense of peace and connection with the environment that he had never experienced before. Additionally, he found a new appreciation for the slower pace of life and the sense of community in the small town. This unexpected change led Alex to personal growth and a new perspective on life.

Surely, change is a storm, both unpredictable and fierce, but amidst the chaos, growth can bloom and push through, making an incredible comeback. It's in the face of change that we are forced to adapt, to learn new skills, to find new passions, and to discover who we truly are. Embrace the change and let it shape you into something even more beautiful.

PRACTICES TO HELP DEAL WITH CHAOS AND CHANGE

Sometimes, when chaos or change happens to us, we want to get out, be alone, or find comfort. Ideas of things that could be comforting or help us deal with the noise, chaos and change are as follows:

1. MEDITATION

The positive effects of meditation on health have been proven scientifically. It's an ideal method in dealing with anxiety, anger, pain, and so on. Joining a meditation or yoga class can help your mind. Don't think that meditation involves simply staring at a wall or listening to recorded meditations. On the contrary, there are so many forms of meditation, from dancing to crying out loud to staring in a flame—just to name a few. If you can't afford to join a meditation class, you could conduct your research on how to go about it yourself. Below are a few forms of meditation and their benefits to get you started.

Meditation is a practice that has been used for centuries to help individuals achieve inner peace and well-being. There are many different forms of meditation, each with its own unique benefits and techniques.

First, there's **mindfulness meditation**. This form of meditation involves paying attention to the present moment and being aware of one's thoughts, feelings, and surroundings. It is a simple yet effective way to reduce stress and anxiety, while also working to improve focus and concentration. Additionally, it can help improve emotional regulation, aiding individuals to feel more in control of their emotions.

Another form of meditation is **transcendental meditation**. This form of meditation involves the use of a mantra, or a sound or word, that is repeated during the meditation session. This can help to quiet the mind and create a sense of calmness. Transcendental meditation has been shown to reduce stress and anxiety, lower blood pressure, and improve overall well-being.

A third form of meditation is **yoga meditation**. This form of meditation is a combination of physical postures and breathing techniques, which can help to reduce stress and tension in the body. It can also help to improve flexibility and balance and has been shown to improve mental and physical well-being.

Additionally, there's also **guided meditation**, which is a form of meditation in which an individual is guided through the meditation process by a teacher or a pre-recorded voice. This can be helpful for individuals who have difficulty focusing or have difficulty quieting their minds. Guided meditation can also be a useful tool for individuals who are new to meditation and are looking for guidance and support.

And finally, there's **loving-kindness meditation**, also known as **metta meditation**, which is a form of meditation that focuses on sending feelings of love. The practice involves repeating phrases or mantras that express love and compassion, such as, "May you be happy; may you be healthy; may you be safe; and may you be at ease."

2. FINDING WHAT WORKS FOR YOU

People tend to find solace and calmness in certain things that become personal to them such that going back to these things during times of chaos in their lives somehow makes them feel better. For some, it's music or a specific place, while for others, it's food or a certain object. So, if you think there's something or somewhere that makes you feel inner peace, then you should stick to them during times of chaos or change.

You may choose to engage in physical activities, such as exercise, yoga, or dancing. Physical activity can release endorphins, which are chemicals in the brain that can improve mood and reduce stress.

You may also find that journaling or talking to a therapist or counselor can help you process your thoughts and feelings and give you a sense of control over the unexpected or sudden changes you may be facing. Additionally, reaching out to friends or loved ones for support can also be beneficial, and being open to asking for help can be a sign of strength.

Ultimately, the key is to be open-minded and try different things to find what works best for you. It may take some time and experimentation, but by being patient and persistent, you will find ways to help you face change or stress more effectively.

3. HYPNOTHERAPY

Hypnotherapy is a therapeutic process that unlocks the power of your unconscious mind. It is a practice to rewire your brain, to overcome old belief patterns, and to heal the wounds of the past. It used to help treat people even with a medical, mental, or psychological disorder or stress. It helps relieve anxieties or coping with traumatic events.

During hypnotherapy, the therapist will guide the individual into a state of deep relaxation and heightened suggestibility, in which they can access the unconscious mind and make positive changes.

One of the main benefits of hypnotherapy is its effectiveness in treating stress and anxiety. Hypnosis can help to reduce the fight or flight response and promote relaxation, which can reduce symptoms of stress and anxiety. Furthermore, hypnotherapy can be used to treat phobias, post-traumatic stress disorder (PTSD), and panic disorder, all of which could manifest during times of extreme and sudden chaotic change.

Hypnotherapy is also used to help individuals quit smoking, lose weight, and overcome other habits and addictions. Many people experiencing negative and chaotic change adopt bad habits to help them cope, which may include smoking, overeating, or allowing themselves to be consumed by other additions. And so, by accessing the unconscious mind, hypnotherapy can help individuals change their thought patterns and behaviors related to these bad habits and behaviors, which can lead to a greater chance of success in overcoming it, as well as dealing with the root cause of the problem.

Additionally, hypnotherapy can be used to help individuals manage chronic pain, such as headaches, back pain, and fibromyalgia, all of which may manifest as physical symptoms in response to negative and chaotic change. As we discussed earlier, when the stress of change remains unaddressed, or when an individual remains in a state of denial rather than acceptance and adaptability, their body may respond to the situation through physical complaints, such as chronic pain. Research suggests that hypnosis can help reduce the perception of pain and improve the individual's ability to cope with it, while also addressing and resolving the root cause of said pain.

Hypnotherapy can also be used to improve self-esteem and confidence. Too often, when an individual experiences negative and chaotic change, their self-esteem takes a hit, especially if this change involves, for example, a job loss, in which the individual is no longer able to provide for their family or successfully fulfill their role or expectations. By accessing the unconscious mind, hypnotherapy can help individuals overcome negative thoughts and beliefs that may be limiting them. It can help individuals to develop a more positive self-image and feel more confident in their abilities.

Hypnotherapy is evidently powerful insofar as it can help individuals overcome a wide range of mental and physical issues. It can be a valuable tool for individuals looking to make positive changes in their lives, and it's important to find a qualified hypnotherapist to guide you through the process.

As a certified master hypnosis coach myself, I can assure you that attending a hypnotherapy session can help you cope with chaos and change. In fact, I recommend that you give it a try.

4. TALKING TO SOMEONE OR A SUPPORT GROUP

If talking helps you cope, then it is important to find someone you trust, a therapist, or a support group. Doing so might help you let go of the mental stress and burden that chaos and change have caused you.

Building and using a support group during difficult times and times of change is crucial for an individual's emotional and mental well-being. A support group can provide a sense of community, belonging, and understanding, which can be essential during times of stress, anxiety, and uncertainty.

One of the most important benefits of a support group is the emotional support that it can provide. Having people who understand what you're going through and who are willing to listen and offer a kind or helpful word can be incredibly valuable. Being able to share your thoughts and feelings with others who understand can help reduce feelings of isolation and loneliness, which can be especially important during difficult times.

A support group can also provide practical support. For example, if you're going through a difficult time and need help with childcare, transportation, or other practical needs, a support group can often help to provide these services. Additionally, having a support group can help to provide resources, such as referrals to professionals, books, or websites that may be helpful to you.

A support group can also help to provide perspective. Having others to talk to who have been through similar experiences can help you see that you're not alone and that others have been able to get through difficult times. They can help you set realistic expectations that ultimately set you up for success. It can also provide you with different perspectives on your situation, which can be helpful when you're feeling stuck or overwhelmed.

During times of change, a support group can provide a sense of continuity and stability. When everything else is changing, having a group of people who are there for you can be incredibly crucial. They can help you navigate the changes, provide a sounding board for your ideas, and help you find the resources you need to make the transition.

Building and using a support group during difficult times and times of change is essential for emotional and mental well-being. Support groups can be found in various forms, such as online groups, self-help groups, therapy groups, and more, and it's important for you to find the one that works best for you and your needs.

Want to be a master of chaos? Implement the pieces of advice provided to you above and see how well you start coping with change and chaos.

Storm

Learn to love the storm and you can cross an ocean.

Part Three

MY STORY: THE GENESIS

Learn to love the storm and you can cross an ocean.

For what it's worth, I appreciate the experiences I've faced and the talents I've developed over time. What is it that people call *learning from experience* and why would you want it to always be smooth sailing?

"Chaos is what we experience in the moments when situations go south, and we are bamboozled with the changes that seem to cause loss of orderliness to a plan or a dream that eventually affects the outcome we wanted. It happens differently for everyone. Chaos makes the reaction of getting hacked off and wheezing prominent until we cool it off." - Me.

Embracing chaos is the opportunity to study something (another part of our existence or cosmos) to avail ourselves of still breathing (being alive), which is the only thing we are left with. Life is a gift wrapped in both good and bad moments to bring the uniqueness of all gifts. You have to identify and study it. You cannot define your life with chaos, weaknesses, or anxiety. You learn how things could work out with your life by not giving up or allowing the chaos to define you.

There are things that will make you more driven than anything in the world. The first thing a newborn does is learn how to live every day to be more knowledgeable than yesterday. The newborn continues to do this every day until old age, hence the phrase *from cradle to grave*. The first thing we all did after birth was learn.

Through much hardship, I have come to learn that the past is meant to be put on the back burner and is not meant to be in our present. Keeping your past in the present stops you from viewing it as history.

Man will be blessed by life but not all blessings come with a smile; some blessings come as lessons for us and others. We all believe that we can achieve greatness. No one wants to be on the bed of failure and sipping from the wine of penury.

You might be thinking about the future in a different way. I thought of my future even when it seemed like I did not have much of it. To grow, you must be alive.

You have chaos in your life to teach you what balance is in the hardest ways and lead you to the ladder of progress.

The worst feeling is existing in a graveyard before actually going six feet below the ground. I refused to do this and instead chose to learn.

Shunning the truth and hushing wisdom is the first thing that takes a real future from us.

I started my life as Sunday child, born on a Sunday morning, but the future looked not bright in those postwar days 1950.

Like every other boy living in the 50s after the war in Linz, Austria, I was faced with the harsh reality. A postwar world is a harsh teacher. It forces you to grow up quickly, leaving behind the innocence of childhood, and making you face the brutal realities of life. It thrusts you into a world of chaos and destruction, forcing you to learn to navigate it to survive. A postwar takes away the luxuries of safety and security and teaches you to be independent and self-sufficient. However, for those of us forced to ensure this arduous life, it at least shapes you into something indestructible, both physically and mentally.

My mother worked in a laboratory and was the solely breadwinner, because my father still was a student of chemistry. The three new family members compelled my parents to put us in a nursing home. I started living there when I turned 18 months and remained until the age of three. Living without my mother's hugs and father's support made me more isolated and self-sufficient than most boys my age, though this neglect has lasting effects.

It wasn't easy gathering the strength to be independent at such a young age; and it was certainly not desirable. However, this was not in my family's control, nor was it in my control. It was something I was forced to adapt to, whether I liked it or not. The situation drove my parents to this decision as they danced to its tune compulsorily for survival. I understand now that I needed to undergo this experience because it helped me when we later moved to Germany.

As with everyone's story, hardship and adversity are necessary for growth.

We followed my father's career path who had a PhD in chemistry. He was constantly moving from one place to another. As a result, I stayed in many places as a kid, which exposed me to a lot of things. I attended an elementary school in Wiesbaden, Wuppertal, Leonding, Austria, and Siegburg, Germany. The best way to survive was to adapt as quickly as possible. I was later forced to attend a Catholic boarding school in Linz, Austria.

If you think things can't get worse, think again.
The hardest part to adapt to was my parents' divorce. I was 12 years old, and the memory still lingers in my mind like it happened yesterday. Still, I managed to adapt. That being said, a difficult thing to adapt to was the side effects of my accent. I went back to Austria after being in Germany. So, my peers didn't appreciate my German accent. The term mobbing was not invented those days….

After the divorce and moving back to Austria/Traun my mother had to work, and I was able to help her in making her job easier. I had to bring out the adult in me at a very young age, preparing and cooking meals, nursing my new-born sister. I wanted to be taken care of but that simply wasn't an option.

I loved my mom so much and admired her. All should be proud of me and so I took another step in life to achieve a high school diploma. My father remarried again, supported me financially and paid hefty for a boarding school in the Austrian Alps, Bad Aussee. An old Nazi officer founded the school. However, prestige is not found in history alone. Many deep-pocketed students attended the school because of its recognition as an easy path into the MATURA (high school diploma).

The good intention of my father was to let me grow up in peace and gain the diploma.

Just arrived I was taken into special custody. 2 fractions fought to catch the NEWBIES.

The "cool fraction" fought with swords and the more conservative ones leaned to the Catholic church. I wanted to join the cool gang .

Anyhow, I did not find the swords in our hands to be educational though.

One of the activities we were instructed to take part in was fighting with swords without anything to protect ourselves from getting hurt or wounded. It was an unhealthy and bloody activity for me to partake in. I got hit and bruised many times. Even as a youngster, I deemed the whole thing stupid and that feeling made my reflexes numb. However, I wanted to be liked by my peers, which is what pushed me to participate in the first place.

I had to isolate myself from all the nonsensical things around me, such as instances in which the boys drank beer and adopted typical German behavior.

To find myself, I had to isolate myself.

After putting up with everything for a year, I dropped out of school and spent the summer working at a factory. For me, schooling ended when I was sixteen. I was already on my own at this time, and this was not a new thing. I actually felt better on my own.

My priority was not to remain in the mindset of a 16-year-old but to conquer the mindset of a 16-year-old by doing things better than boys my age, even though I could not afford school at that period of my life. I needed to find my path.

Was it risky? Yes. Was it worth it? Yes. Did I wish for a life like that? Nope.

No young boy would have wished for that kind of hardship while growing up. However, chaos taught me what no one taught me in school, and I developed through the four walls of chaos and its complications. I would have wished for a peaceful life, but I was not in a position to wish for that. Truth be told, there was nothing peaceful about my life.

Rewind to the teenage years

I was a tall guy that looked older for his age. Some of the female teachers fell in love with me. They even promoted me to join them at summer camp for young kids ranging from the ages of 10-16. Part of the benefits of their generosity was that I was paid by the government and put in the position of a supervisor for those kids. I enjoyed the experience, and I loved the company.

When I turned 17, I joined the Austrian military, because they allowed me to continue my education on an evening economic school. I learned that military drill is not my path and managed to leave in honor after surviving a press scandal that put them in peril.

At 18, I put myself on a budget to get my driver's license. I was hired as a commercial accountant in a big industrial painting company. My job description was calculating the salaries of workers and taking the cash to the working sites. I found it challenging to make the calculations of the wages correctly and deduct the money for insurance and tax from the wages. I did not anticipate this, but I braced for the unforeseen circumstances that life in its chaotic nature might bring to my doorstep. I knew that opportunities were to be seized, and whenever it seemed like there was no opportunity, I knew I had to create one. I lived for the challenge and worked through it.

The company was magnanimous. I was provided with a 6 – cylinder, Rover 3.0 and an awesome salary for my age and education. The company thought that I could become the next commercial director as that position was vacant due to the fact that the former commercial director was fired based on his corrupted mindset. The company couldn't tolerate a commercial director who was corrupt. Notwithstanding, I did not have the intention of staying in the company. I placed an ad in a local newspaper and got two offers later from a retail bank and an advertising agency.

Life is not worthy of being stuck in one place. We all believe in a good life, but no one wants a hard life. Your world does not have to end when you log out of your computer at the office. Someone has to take on the risky parts of life. Life does not stay in one place; it is always putting people on the street and placing others in positions of power.

What do you believe? If it is yourself, are you going to cope differently through the difficulties?

Some were born with the golden spoon and extremely lucky, but knowledge and own achievements is often what keeps them in that position for long.

You can successfully wield power with knowledge. When you foolishly find yourself at the top of having a better life, you will foolishly find yourself back on the streets of wherever you are from if you are even that lucky. Chaos brought me up and made me self-driven and hopeful for the best in an odd world that does not give a damn about who eats and who does not.

I could not stay at that industrial painting company because my boss would not have gotten the opportunity to employ better heads that were capable of skyrocketing what he stood for and the figures in his account. I needed to move and move until I got there. There was a journey ahead and I needed vigor for it. So, I believed that the next step was to join the advertising agency in Linz.

I jumped on it like a disc jockey and started working there as a copywriter and a correspondent for an international network. It was a new challenge to show prowess amid the chaos. I had to become as optimistic as I could. To be candid, I never did anything like copywriting before and did not want to show any weakness to the company.

Your environment has a way of making you feel either comfortable or uncomfortable with yourself and others. *Remembering what I did next makes me smile at the 18-year-old me.*

I started feeling like a king. I made and saw myself as a king and no one dared bring me down. I became stronger by learning through the hardships I faced while growing up. I proceeded to paint my rented studio black, and I acted like an ingenious creative head. Little did I know that I had just given myself away. All the young people event the very affluent ones in Linz tried to join me.

I did not like the fact that my job at the advertising agency was getting boring. It made me put my ear to the ground for another opportunity. My dream was not to get stuck in a rented studio nor work for the agency until retirement. I wanted to drive an PORSCHE around town.

I made my calculations, and the number I arrived at was never going to let me stay. I would have to work 30 years more in Linz to afford a Porsche. If I was to add that to my age as a boy, then I would be driving my dream car at the age of 49. I had to leave to look for a better paying job with more interesting clients. Being ambitiously in tune with the voice in my head made me become futuristically aware of steps to take. I produced an innovative approach to the chaos. I had an idea of buying 50 toy plastic boxes that resembled safes.

I locked my address and mobile number in the toy -safe. I wrote a concise letter that entailed my achievements over the years, my talents, and my skills, and found the perfect spot to put the letter. I believed that there would be someone nosy and talented enough to open the safe and track me down. The challenge for the receiver was to play and find the right combination to open the safe box.

The response of my first direct mail to the leading agencies in Germany and Austria was overwhelming. What comes next was not a dream but a risk that came with a result.

There will always be a price for falling and for rising. You decide the price you want to pay through the chaotic moments for the living because the world is not going to stop if you stop chasing your dream.

The world will not delay its rotational movement around its axis because you stopped learning from the chaos that exists around you. The world keeps revolving around the sun to bring seasons to your existence.

To master it means not to dive into the river of obscurity and low self-esteem; it is a long dive that might take away your strength and leave you regretting your decision. Take a risk that can be seen as childish. You cannot die by taking that step. If you fail, you will learn from it and if you get lucky enough to receive success in your home, you have worked for it, and you must enjoy it.

I was called upon from Hamburg to Vienna. I spent eight weeks traveling around and my traveling expenses were on my potential employers. I was asked a common question by every employer and I gave a salary range that was perfect for me. The young fool was rejected by them, and I was downcast for a bit; my value is too high for them. I must believe in myself more and be proud of myself.

Afterwards, I found another possible employer and was interviewed for a position. I got a job as a copywriter in Solingen, Germany. My salary was three times what it was in Austria. I felt the need to pay more attention to work and became more diligent. I know what it meant to be climbing the ladder and not looking down. I became more hardworking, and it really improved my productivity. I did it without having doubts in my life. I kept working and improved on my time management. My employers were happy enough to raise my salary after nine months of my employment at the agency.

I did not stop hustling. After six months, I worked for a client who ran a big ESSO agency. I did direct mail for him, and it gave me the ground I needed to be on good terms with the boss.

Everyone wanted to work directly with the main boss.

I loved knocking aggressively on the door of opportunity. I refused to let procrastination cuddle me as a boy, taking the necessary chances at changing things by accepting the things that surrounded my upbringing.

Missing Arm

The "Missing Arm" Concept

Run away, you cup of penury. I have heard of your magical feet and your stubborn nature. Let everyone in heaven and earth bear witness today. I will never allow myself to drink from you even if I will lose an arm.

The missing arm of a human being is lack of an idea that marks the end of his foundational problem and control over the sense of pride that he only has the strength to push himself into success. It is good to be independent, but you must also note that people are needed and your humility are needed.

The underground network of the afflicted and lifestyle hinders the vision of many that has created a chasm between the rich and the poor. Forgetting the past is different from learning from the past and is different from prepping for the first moment of your present that will lead to the future of the lineage that is yet to come. If you do not try to get the path to reach our missing arm, you might end up living your whole existence on the planet with that missing arm.

The riches and the better standard of living we look for is not going to come to fruition unless we usher it into this world (our lives). Wealth cannot stand alone; it needs to compliment an individual.

Seeing into the realm of truth and persistence will make you grow a missing arm and still find a more befitting one as you develop your mind (the land that needs to be watered).

The barren mind has agreed to be a slave to the chaos roaring and walking majestically around it. You fear the wild cat that can be tamed and put in a zoo. Instead, I want you to embrace it and pet it. The faces it keeps showing you will change, and it will keep wanting to break free from your grasp. Do not give up on petting it. You are meant to be the master of it and not the other way round. I embraced what happened and I lived through it.

I am still alive and still facing my own lion, but I have become a man of courage because of it, although it keeps trying to get out from the den I have put it in. What makes us different is how much success we give and how long it lasts for.

Envying is not the right channel to yield to in a moment in which you are seeking after the missing arm. Nowadays, people are so frightened of the lion; they are constantly pressing the panic button in their minds. They either give up or develop anxiety by basing their future on their weaknesses and not their strengths. I became what I am today not because I learned from fear or anxiety, but because I choose to embrace the place and situation I was born in, which I believed couldn't hold me back from manifesting. For some, they have pride that cannot be turned into ambition or anything fruitful. It's important to also note that the belief is not something that was simply handed to me. Instead, it was something I had to work to cultivate so I could finally change my situation.

Never Stop Searching
I still keep looking for my "missing arm". First, I found one missing arm when I worked at the ad agency. However, a salary is not

going to make anyone rich, but it can give you peace of mind. You can make contributions and invest in things that you believe that have a prospect and if it fails, you are in serious trouble with your family.

The world needs to understand that many people praise those who have found their missing arms rather than sitting down to discover it for themselves. The best teacher is life and part of this is all the chaos in it. You must be strong enough mentally and physically to get yourself out of the wrong environment.

Listen to Your Inner Voice

People will give suggestions that will confuse you rather than give you direction. I grew up knowing that the only person that could understand me and my dreams well enough was me. I would benefit the most if this body gets the comfort it has been looking for.

Voices from outside cannot be as resounding as the ones in your head. You know yourself best and you know that if you give up on yourself right now, you will be the one to feel the failure that clutches your mind. Think about it like this. Listening to your inner voice is like tuning into a radio station only you have access to. It's a channel where your intuition speaks, your inner wisdom whispers, and your true self sings. It's provides guidance and direction, that when tuned into, it can lead you to the path of self-discovery and fulfillment. So, put on your listening ears, and let your inner voice be your compass.

That being said, listening to your inner voice is one of the most important things you can do for yourself. It is the voice of your intuition, your inner wisdom, and it is always guiding you towards your true purpose in life. It is the voice that reminds you of who you are, and what you are capable of achieving. It is the voice that tells you when something is not right, and when something is worth fighting for.

Listening to your inner voice is not always easy. In fact, the noise of the world around us may completely drown out the sound, but nonetheless, it is a skill that can be developed with practice and patience. It requires you to be present in the moment, to quiet your mind, and to listen to the voice within. It requires you to be honest with yourself, to admit when you are wrong, and to take responsibility for your actions. It requires you to be true to yourself, to stand up for what you believe in, and to live your life with integrity.

When you listen to your inner voice, you will find that your life becomes more meaningful and fulfilling. You will find that you make better decisions, and that you are able to achieve your goals and dreams. You will find that you are more resilient and that you are able to handle challenges with grace and ease.

Listening to your inner voice also helps you build better relationships, as you are able to communicate your needs and boundaries clearly, and to empathize with others. It allows you to be more authentic in your interactions, and to build deeper connections with the people in your life.

However, note that to effectively listen to your inner voice, you must be willing to take risks, to step out of your comfort zone, and to trust in yourself. This may require you to let go of old patterns and embrace new ways of being. But with each step you take, you will find that you are becoming more and more in tune with your inner voice, and that you are becoming more and more true to yourself.

Listening to your inner voice is an essential aspect of self-discovery and personal growth. It is the voice that guides you towards your true purpose and helps you to make decisions that serve you best. You will find that your life becomes more meaningful and fulfilling, and that you are able to navigate the chaos of the world.

But surely, this is easier said than done. What techniques can we implement to ensure that the voice we're listening to is authentic, insofar as it is coming from ourselves, rather than a mixture of others' thoughts and feelings about what we ought to do.

Listening to your inner voice instead of that of others requires both self-awareness and discipline, which can be developed and improved upon by practicing mindfulness techniques involving being present in the moment and paying close attention to your thoughts, emotions, and bodily sensations. This can help you determine when your inner voice is speaking, and the voices that are not your own are drowning it out. Moreover, setting aside quiet time for yourself each day to reflect—possibly through journaling or meditation—can also be helpful in developing self-awareness.

Furthermore, discerning the difference between your own thoughts and feelings and those of others is another way of ensuring your voice comes out on top. You can achieve this by questioning the source of your thoughts and feelings, rather than simply accepting them at face value and assuming that they are coming from a true and genuine place. This can help you identify when you are being influenced by others, and when you are following the guidance of your inner voice. Finally, it's important to set boundaries and be assertive in expressing your needs and wants. This can be difficult, especially if you are used to putting others' needs before your own, but it's a crucial step in learning to listen to your inner voice.

This kind of mindset requires more than prayers to make a comeback. In this life, when an opportunity is lost, do not waste time regretting it. Live on and realize that you are the only one with the power to improve your existence. You cannot afford to waste that life on regrets that will make you loose the vigor to continue with your journey.

You also cannot run from the things that you must experience. You have to go through a variety of experiences so you can share your developed strength with others. You owe it to yourself and your family to provide a good life, and this can happen if you turn your energy into looking for your missing arm. Take the risk. You either win and smile or lose and learn what must be learned.

I know change is an inevitable part of life, and it can be difficult to navigate, especially when it comes unexpectedly. I've faced far too many sudden changes to count, but every time, I addressed them head on, and I refused to let them consume me. It is natural to feel uncertain, anxious, and even scared when faced with change. However, running away from change is not the solution. Instead, it is important to face change head-on and to learn how to adapt to it.

Facing change allows us to grow and develop as individuals. It challenges us to step out of our comfort zones and try new things. It forces us to confront our fears and to learn how to overcome them. It helps us become more resilient and develop a greater sense of self-awareness. By facing change, we are able to learn new skills, gain new perspectives, and see the world in a different light.

Facing change also allows us to take control of our lives. When we run away from change, we are giving up control and allowing the change to control us. However, when we face change, we can make conscious choices about how we want to respond to it. We can choose how we want to adapt and make the change work for us. This allows us to have a sense of agency and empowerment, which is essential for our mental and emotional well-being.

Also, when we run away from change, we miss out on the potential opportunities that the change may bring. For example, a job loss may seem like the end of the world, but it may also be an opportunity to find a job that is a better fit, to start a new business, or to step into a new career path. When we face change, we can see the potential opportunities that it may bring and consequently, we are able to seize them.

The image of having only a secured, peaceful, or calm lifestyle is always going to be quixotic. Change is bound to happen, and you have to acknowledge it, learn about it, and create your way out of the change. Running away from change does not mean that it stopped existing in your life. Chaos is needed to value peace. It is part of the galaxy that you are existing in, and you are never going to keep denying that you have to face it now or later. Being optimistic in turmoil is necessary when looking for your missing arm.

When we face change, we open ourselves up to gratitude and appreciation for the present moment. This allows us to find joy and contentment in the present, rather than dwelling on the past or worrying about the future. When we run away from change, on the other hand, we force our minds to focus on what we have lost or what we are afraid of losing.

Opportunities are invited through intelligence and a good attitude. Losing one means losing a leg, and when opportunity comes knocking on the door, you have to crawl to open it.

Covid-19 and the Unconscious Mind

You can never stop looking for your missing arm because as you grow and develop, you will need another missing one to complete your growth. You have to gain exposure from those around you. No situation stops you from looking for your missing arm. *I still looked for another missing arm during the Covid-19 lockdown. I studied hypnotherapy and am now a licensed hypnotherapist (NGH, US, Switzerland, Germany) and a yoga and meditation teacher.*

There is no hindrance to looking for your missing arm. Simply avoid laziness and procrastination. You need to challenge yourself to keep pushing forward and looking for the things you could do next. But how? Let's look at some tangible pieces of advice you can implement to ensure you find your missing arm—or, in other words, the missing pieces of yourself you may have lost along the journey of life.

Covid-19 has swept through our lives, leaving behind a trail of uncertainty, isolation, and loss in its wake. It has forced us to redefine ourselves, to let go of the familiar, and to embrace the unknown. And in this process, we may have lost pieces of our identity. But we must rise from the ashes, and learn to rebuild ourselves, stronger and more resilient than before.

First, it is important to recognize that it is normal to feel this way during such a challenging and unprecedented time, and to know that there are ways to find and reconnect with those missing pieces of yourself.

One way to start looking for the missing pieces of yourself or your missing arm is to take a step back and reflect on what has changed in your life since the pandemic began. This can include changes in your daily routine, relationships, and sense of purpose. By acknowledging these changes, you can start to identify what parts of yourself may be missing and what you may need to reconnect with.

Furthermore, as I've discussed earlier, it is important to allow yourself to try new things. The pandemic has forced many of us to alter our routines, which many of us may have originally perceived as negative, but when we re-frame our way of thinking, we can begin to understand that a change in our regular routines allows us to integrate new hobbies and activities into our daily lives. This can help you find new passions and reconnect with parts of yourself that may have been forgotten. For example, you can try a new hobby like painting, cooking, or writing, or you can take a class online to learn a new skill.

It is also important to focus on self-care during this time. The pandemic has brought about a lot of stress and anxiety, as it is a major change that we've all been forced to undergo. However, doing the things that bring you happiness and satisfaction can be beneficial in helping you reconnect with the missing parts of yourself. For instance, you can spend time in nature, listen to music, read a book, or engage in any other activity that may bring you any semblance of joy. This is also a good opportunity to practice self-compassion, as this will allow you to find your missing arm and reconnect with the pieces of yourself you may have lost along the way.

Since the pandemic has brought about great deals of uncertainty, it is important to be kind and understanding towards yourself as you navigate these changes. It is imperative to remember that it is normal to feel lost or disconnected at times, and to remind yourself that it is okay to not have all the answers right now. All that matters is that you remain hardworking, dedicated, and adopt a mindset that allows you to move forward rather than stay stagnant in the face of change. Remember, we are all in this together.

Mastering the Chaos: An Art You Never Stop Learning

The ticking time bomb that was my life needed to be diffused but no one was around to do it for me. *In critical stages of upbringing, I had no father to pat me on the back and no mother to kiss me on the head. I had two parents, but they were prisoners of their own limitations.*

That being said, I learned not to blame anyone for my failures or for being a lackadaisical student to the teachings of the chaos of my realm. I tore the first ticket and kept the piece in my pocket. Pride struck me with its fist in my face. I received the first blow of and it bruised me. I never knew what ego was and why I had the opportunity to feel it as a kid. It made me feel like I had something though and a friend to help me reject the wrong ideas and to become a good student.

Mastering the chaos is much more than resilience.

Resilience has for me a passive approach. You are able to endure the chaos surrounding you. If you train yourself to master the chaos, you will see the chances "the missing arms" on your journey.

When I look back, nothing was as bad to me as losing all the time. The world and your family will categorize you as a loser and you will start to keep your head down as a result. This is something I did when I was a kid. The other kids played and laughed. They scampered around the yards. I was not much of a playful person, but I understood the feeling of intense happiness, even in the midst of calamity. But fun was not my priority; it was not enough reason to keep myself in one state for a long time.

The wise ones that can mix fun and reasoning will leave the others who cannot at the level they are until there is no fun left in them anymore. The world needs to know that there is a lesson in everything, whether it's happiness, success, wealth, productivity, or innovation. I did that to prepare my mind with a soft landing. The other aspect of life that we see as negative is actually a tunnel for valor.

The real convocation is when you walk through and past the tunnel. Note that I am not providing reasons to love negativity, but rather urging that the world needs to be prepared to accept that negativity is part of our success. Positivity takes all the credit for itself. Success has its villa on the highest ground. Failure, on the other hand, is the real estate agent that makes houses available for people to live. As wicked as it is, it has the fame that makes everyone, even those in the villa, speak of it. They do not like to have an encounter with failure, but it makes them realize the importance of being mentally strong and ready to push through to reach the villa they are living in.

The real teacher is not living up there with them. The real teacher is living at the base of the villa and expanding its estate. It keeps an eye on everyone that is on the ground and visits the villa to check up on those living there. It wants to breed the masters of its pets and not the ones that fear them. Risky business is what failure likes the most; the invitation to the VIP spot is gained by learning the game and mastering it.

Learn to Swim

I founded my first agency at twenty. For some people, the real problem isn't taking risks, rather it's recognizing the right ones to take. This is primarily because not all risks are meant to be taken no matter how far you have gone. That is the primary reason for why I started my agency, GBK+Partner (Gassner, Bachem, Kubiak, and Partner). I started pulling every string attached to the missing arm and I finally managed to place a big PR story in the leading ad journal, and it was a one-pager. I knew that some risks are not meant to be taken alone and other people are required for success. When it came to creating my first agency, I needed to go through it with the help of other people. I knew failure and its pests were lurking around the corner. I noticed that the people I brought together to create the agency were different in one way to me: I was the only breadwinner while the other people waited for jobs. I knew that my drive was greater than theirs because they had mentally limited themselves already; however, the credit was not all mine. The difficult situations I'd faced in my lifetime prepared me to adopt such a mindset and such a powerful will to succeed.

I was only twenty years old, but I pulled the agency out of the depths of my being to ensure I was never going to repeat classes anymore. I wanted to become the master of my emotions. Chaos had the potential to affect my emotions negatively, but I never gave it that authority over my feelings and life.

Socrates once said, "Education is the kindling of a flame, not the filling of a vessel."

I dropped out of school, not out of my dreams. The difference between the ones that make it after dropping out and the ones that don't is whether the dream is kept alive and whether the individual chases it.

The experiences of the two lives have made me wise enough to make decisions about certain things with my eyes closed.

Pythagoras said, "Man, know thyself." It made me feel the urge to see through the pain of being in situations of despair. You must understand yourself first before you can help anyone else see themselves for who they really are.

Regardless, I took my time and continued what I knew best

I was hired after three months by a famous advertising agency in Düsseldorf as a senior copywriter. I worked for the big clients in Germany. It was a very professional atmosphere. I was working directly with an art director at that time.

I allowed the truth to set me free. I was a dropout that never had the experience to be where I was, and I was working with professionals with a sound educational background. I encouraged myself to push through all issues that I faced with the words that my mind still replays every time I face a new challenge, "If I went to school, I would not have got to where I am right now."

Those who were my age were in school, while I tried to move myself into a professional arena that graduates were also trying to enter. What mattered most was the fact that I could read and write. Education is not only achieved within the four walls of a classroom, but rather, education can be gained all around you.

My story began when I moved into a fancy apartment next to the art wizard, Joseph Beuys in Düsseldorf/Drakestreet. Often we had a friendly chat over the garden wall and I never forget his felt hat that he never missed.

I loved the agency, but I saw the fact that I had to work with my head placed on the train track while my creative director always showed up drunk at noon. I saw it as a tangible reason to be vexed.

Ride the Wave of Opportunity

This propelled me to look for another opportunity. I was working my heart out while someone else was drinking to a stupor. I gave all of me to increase productivity. I kept looking for the next missing arm and I found it at 22—at least I thought I did—after a notable boutique agency hired me as a senior copywriter with the aim to be the succeeding group head. However, I found its atmosphere too top-notch for me, too defined, inhospitable, and because of that, I quit my job there in hopes of going elsewhere.

I was hired right in the agency next door as a creative -group head. WerbeCompany merged with WERBE ESSEN and that gave the ground for them to work for clients like Coca-Cola / Germany, big pharma, Scholl sandals and other famous brand names. We shot television commercials for Scholl sandals in South Africa and commercials in the Bahamas for Paradise bed wear. At this point, I made money like never before.

I got more and more motivated by my success and it landed me in the position of (creative) director when I was just 24 years old. One thing I didn't let into my head was pride and self-satisfaction. I continued to push harder and became more comfortable with working harder. This landed me in the hands of *head-hunters. I knew that I needed to seek another missing arm because I wanted to grab another part of the mountain where I knew success resided.*

The reason why the missing arm is a necessity is so that it can get you to a higher position. You need as many arms as possible to get you there; the one you are still holding onto might start to quiver after holding onto something for you for so long. And so, you need to keep climbing and collecting those arms to get you higher.

When I turned 26, I got an offer that was way better than any other offer I'd been presented with at the time. I could not resist it. Success called on me all the way from its villa. The leading agency in Munich was on the lookout for a genius creative star for their biggest unit: Peugeot, pharmacy, lotto, a big insurance company, and government accounts. I became responsible for thirty creative people, which doubled my salary. I had to move to Munich to grasp the fresh flesh of success and stick to it.

I worked overnight and won over an increasing number of hulking business deals for the agency, DFS+R Dorland, with the help of my team.

Whenever you are looking for a missing arm and you can see value come forth from your search, you can't waste time procrastinating.

The Butterfly Effect

The butterfly effect is a concept in chaos theory that states that small changes in initial conditions can have large effects on the outcome of a complex system. This principle is often used to describe the unpredictability of weather patterns, but it can also be applied to social and economic systems. In these systems, seemingly small actions or events can have far-reaching consequences.

Research has shown that even minor changes in behavior or decision-making can have significant impacts on outcomes. For example, a study found that offering financial incentives to employees for exercising led to an increase in productivity and a decrease in healthcare costs. Another study showed that small interventions, such as reminders and incentives, can lead to significant increases in organ donation rates.

This highlights the importance of awareness in decision-making and behavior. By being mindful of our actions and the potential outcomes, we can make intentional choices that have positive impacts on ourselves and others. This involves being present in the moment and taking responsibility for our thoughts and actions.

Embracing Chaos with the Butterfly Effect: A Case Study

The butterfly effect teaches us that small actions can have big consequences, and this can be a powerful tool for embracing chaos in our lives. Here are some specific examples and guidance on how to apply the butterfly effect in our daily lives:

- Start with small changes: We often feel overwhelmed by the chaos in our lives, but the butterfly effect reminds us that small changes can make a big difference. For example, instead of trying to completely overhaul our diet, we can start by making one healthy choice at a time. Over time, these small changes can lead to big improvements in our health and wellbeing.

- Be mindful of our actions: The butterfly effect also reminds us to be mindful of our actions and the potential impact they can have. For example, a kind word or gesture to a stranger can create a ripple effect of positivity that spreads far beyond that one interaction.

- Embrace the unexpected: The butterfly effect also teaches us that chaos can be a source of creativity and innovation. By embracing the unexpected, we can open ourselves up to new possibilities and experiences. For example, trying a new hobby or taking a different route to work can lead to unexpected connections and opportunities.

- Focus on what we can control: While chaos may be unpredictable, we can still focus on what we can control in our lives. By setting small goals and taking intentional actions, we can create a sense of order and purpose amidst the chaos. For example, setting a daily intention or practicing gratitude can help us stay grounded and focused on what truly matters.

Living in the present moment is a critical aspect of living a fulfilling life. The butterfly effect, which is the idea that small actions can have significant consequences, illustrates the importance of being present in the moment. When we are fully aware of our surroundings and conscious of our actions, we can make more deliberate and impactful choices. It's crucial to note that living in the past or the future doesn't provide any significant benefits, and it can actually hinder our ability to make meaningful decisions in the present.

Living in the present moment means being aware of our thoughts, emotions, and physical sensations as they arise. It means paying attention to our surroundings and engaging with the world around us. When we are fully present, we can notice things we may have overlooked otherwise, and this allows us to make more informed decisions.

Living in the past or the future, on the other hand, can be a significant source of stress and anxiety. When we ruminate on past events or worry about future outcomes, we are not fully present in the moment. This can lead to negative thought patterns that can affect our overall well-being.

To ensure that we are aware of our surroundings and living in the present, we can engage in mindfulness practices. Mindfulness involves paying attention to the present moment without judgment. This can be achieved through various techniques, such as meditation, deep breathing, or simply focusing on our surroundings.

One technique that can help us overcome negative thoughts that pull us to the past is cognitive restructuring. This involves challenging negative thoughts and replacing them with more positive ones. For example, if we find ourselves ruminating on a past event, we can challenge the thought by asking ourselves if there is evidence to support it. If there isn't any evidence, we can replace the thought with a more positive one.

To master the skill of living in the present moment in the face of chaos, we can practice mindfulness regularly. This involves setting aside time each day to engage in mindfulness exercises. We can also incorporate mindfulness into our daily routine by paying attention to our surroundings and being fully present in our interactions with others.

Another way to master this skill is to practice self-compassion. When we are kind and compassionate to ourselves, we are more likely to be present in the moment and make more deliberate choices. We can practice self-compassion by being kind to ourselves when we make mistakes, acknowledging our emotions without judgment, and taking care of ourselves physically, emotionally, and mentally.

Living in the present moment is crucial in relation to the butterfly effect. When we are fully present, we can make more deliberate and impactful choices that can have significant consequences. Living in the past or the future doesn't provide any significant benefits, and it can actually hinder our ability to make meaningful decisions in the present. To ensure that we are aware of our surroundings and living in the present, we can engage in mindfulness practices and practice self-compassion. By mastering this skill, we can lead a more fulfilling and meaningful life.

Moreover, the butterfly effect can help reframe our mindset and empower us to face chaos head-on. By recognizing that small actions can have big consequences, we can take intentional steps towards creating positive change. This can help us overcome hardships related to chaos, such as feeling overwhelmed or powerless in the face of uncertainty. By focusing on what we can control and taking small steps towards our goals, we can navigate rough waters with greater confidence and resilience. The butterfly effect reminds us that even in the midst of chaos, we have the power to create positive change in ourselves and in the world around us.

One person who successfully applied the concepts of chaos theory and the butterfly effect to gain control of their life is Jane, a 32-year-old entrepreneur who was struggling to get her business off the ground.

Jane had always been passionate about starting her own business, but despite her best efforts, she couldn't seem to make any progress. She had tried every strategy she could think of, from networking to advertising to changing her product line, but nothing seemed to work.

One day, while browsing the internet for inspiration, Jane stumbled upon an article about chaos theory and the butterfly effect. Intrigued, she began to read more about how small changes can have big effects and how seemingly random events can shape the course of our lives.

As she read, Jane began to realize that she had been approaching her business all wrong. Instead of trying to force her way to success, she needed to embrace the idea of small changes and let the chaos work in her favor.

With this new mindset, Jane began to take small steps to improve her business. She started by rebranding her company with a new logo and a catchy tagline. She also began to attend more networking events and reached out to new contacts on social media.

At first, it seemed like these small changes weren't making much of a difference. But then, one day, Jane received an email from a potential client who had seen her new logo and was interested in working with her. From there, things began to snowball. Jane's social media following grew, and she started receiving more inquiries from interested customers.

As Jane continued to make small changes and embrace the chaos, her business began to flourish. She hired new employees and expanded her product line, and before she knew it, she was running a successful company that had exceeded her wildest dreams.

Looking back, Jane realized that the butterfly effect had played a huge role in her success. If she had never stumbled upon that article about chaos theory, she might never have changed her approach to her business. And if she hadn't taken those small steps, she might never have landed that first big client that set everything in motion.

Today, Jane is a firm believer in the power of the butterfly effect and the importance of embracing the chaos in our lives.

She encourages others to take small steps toward their goals and to be open to the unexpected opportunities that can arise from even the smallest changes.

Jane's success story is a testament to the power of chaos theory and the butterfly effect. By making small changes and letting the chaos work in her favor, she was able to gain control of her life and achieve her dreams. This is a lesson that we can all learn from, whether we are entrepreneurs or simply looking to improve our lives in other ways.

The Butterfly Effect, Chaos Theory, and Crisis Management
The butterfly effect and chaos theory have important implications for crisis management, as they highlight the potential for small events to trigger larger and more unpredictable outcomes. By understanding these concepts, individuals and organizations can better prepare for and respond to crises, whether they be natural disasters, cyberattacks, or financial crises.

One example of the butterfly effect in crisis management is the case of the 2003 Northeast blackout, which was triggered by a single software bug in an Ohio control room. This bug caused a chain reaction that led to a cascading power outage across much of the Northeastern United States and Canada, affecting over 50 million people and causing billions of dollars in damages.[5] This illustrates how a small, seemingly insignificant

---

5　National Geographic. (2013, August 14). 2003 blackout: What caused the massive outage 10 years ago? National Geographic Society. https://www.nationalgeographic.com/news/2013/8/130814-2003-blackout-power-grid-cause-electricity-technology/

event can have major consequences in a complex system, such as the power grid.

Another example of the butterfly effect in crisis management is the case of the 2008 financial crisis, which was triggered by a complex web of interconnected factors, including subprime mortgage lending, securitization, and the proliferation of complex financial instruments. As Nassim Taleb argues in his book "The Black Swan," the financial crisis was the result of a series of small, seemingly random events that combined to create a large and unpredictable outcome.[6] This highlights how a lack of understanding of the nonlinear and dynamic nature of complex systems can lead to catastrophic consequences in times of crisis.

Chaos theory also has important implications for crisis management, as it emphasizes the importance of feedback loops and nonlinear relationships between variables. For example, in the context of a natural disaster such as a hurricane, the impacts of the storm can be highly dependent on factors such as wind speed, water temperature, and atmospheric pressure. These factors interact with one another in complex and nonlinear ways, making it difficult to predict the precise impact of the storm on a given area.[7]

To apply these concepts to our own lives, we can take steps to better understand the complex systems that we interact with on a daily basis. For example, in the context of financial

____

6 Taleb, N. N. (2007). The black swan: The impact of the highly improbable. Random House.

7 Lorenz, E. N. (1996). The essence of chaos. University of Washington Press.

planning, we can recognize the importance of diversification and risk management, as a small event such as a market downturn can have major consequences for our portfolios. Similarly, in the context of cybersecurity, we can recognize the importance of regularly updating our software and taking steps to secure our personal information, as a small vulnerability in our digital systems can have major consequences for our privacy and security.

The butterfly effect and chaos theory have important implications for crisis management, as they highlight the potential for small events to trigger larger and more unpredictable outcomes in complex systems. By recognizing the nonlinear and dynamic nature of these systems and taking steps to prepare for and respond to crises, we can mitigate the impacts of unpredictable events in our own lives and in the world around us.

Have you ever stopped to think about the power of a butterfly's wings? How the slightest flutter can create a ripple effect that travels across oceans and continents, influencing the course of events in ways we could never predict? It's a phenomenon known as the butterfly effect, and it reminds us that small actions can have a big impact. So when life throws us hardship and adversity, let's remember the butterfly's wings and how they can help us overturn seas, overcome obstacles, and thrive. Because even in the face of chaos, our actions can create a ripple effect that changes the world.

Prepare yourself to overturn the sea

Prepare Yourself to Overturn the Seas

This is a condition that can be turned into an opportunity. Create the atmosphere that can bring you back into the comfortable room you go home to sleep every night. You have to be an opportunity-seeker, but the other option is to be an opportunist.

Putting yourself in a place where it becomes easier for success to locate you makes it an enjoyable ride and makes it less challenging because you already know the other side of life: hardship.

I was told that Ogilvy Vienna was looking for a creative star. I knew what the situation looked like, and I knew what I had to do with it. I threw my hand into the sea to turn the water and saw that it was already foamy, so I gave it my price.

I said, "One million Austrian Schilling. Net cash and car, expense account, and all the nitty gritty. Think of the year 79 !! The foamy sea already felt the impact of my hand and they agreed to pay me that amount in 1979. I liked it, but finally, I listened to the siren of Schmid-Preissler in Gruenwald/ Munich, who was the top boutique brand agency in Germany at that time. I proceeded to take the position of the new creative partner of Schmid Preissler, an agency with first-rate clients.

Turning the sea came with some other benefits, like residing in an appealing château, having my own secretary, assistants, copywriters, photographers, and chauffeur that drove me in a Mercedes Benz 500 to presentations and client meetings. Everything was grand. The salary was impressive, and I had a really good relationship with the owner of the agency.

I fell in love with my assistant and things went wrong. We divorced. This turned the sea red, and I had to remove my hand from it. The once good relationship turned sour, and I could not control its speed. I wanted another sea to turn; my head-hunter kept calling my phone.

The wind was blowing in another direction and J.W Thompson knew where it was headed. Another position as executive creative director opened up and they were searching for someone who was skilled enough to stabilize the big clients that the company had, the list starting with Kraft, Ford, and De Beers Diamond. The wind was prepared to blow me to Frankfurt, Germany.

I went to Madison Ave, New York, USA to improve my English and to make it possible for me to adapt to such an international environment. I was in the EPICENTER of the advertising world. I took part in an international rising star program, and I was trained on the job alongside famous colleagues. My greatest achievement in N.Y. was to help them win the pitch for the US ARMY account.

Recognizing the Devil's Show

So, to turn the seas, you need to work on your relationship with others. You cannot do anything with others. You have to build a good relationship with others while still setting boundaries to avoid any devil's show from the people beneath you. By doing so, you will give many people assurance of humility, focus, and respect.

Chaos Management and the Chaos of Life

I gained another insight into my chaos management. It's never easy to begin with these techniques but it pays in the long run and that's why I'm sharing my experiences and learnings I applied in making it go in my favor by simplifying things.

When I left for Frankfurt, Germany, I was met with a very hostile aura radiating from those around me. I was responsible for the largest unit with all major clients with noteworthy contribution to the agency. My co-workers had a problem with my age; they felt that I was too young, unqualified, and an Austrian fool, which was the motive of their campaign.

They thought it was all some serendipity that I found myself in that position and they remembered how long it took them and the age they were when they reached a position and a pay check much lower than mine.. From this, I learned that you need to create your path even when all odds are stacked against you. This was not an easy feat for me. This was something that involved much failure, but it was something that I was able to achieve nonetheless, and something that you can achieve, as well. It simply requires dedication and hard work, even when the odds are not in your favor.

As much as I was driven and thorough at what I do, I saw others being misled by their emotions, which were created by crisis in their lives that they had not mastered. Yet, they looked down on a young guy that never had anyone to look after him, to show him love, or to hug him when he needed it at nights he slept without food or shelter before he could get himself together. I knew what I had to do and how hard it was going to be for me. I knew how to turn the seas.

I applied love and respect. I acted like we knew each other better and ignored the snubs and replies that were cold with a smile.

I was not there for them, but I was in the agency with them for the same reason: creating the best advertisement for clients. It had been a long time coming for me, and I could not let the frosty atmosphere make me run away from what I was called for. Valor and technique are essential in turning the seas.

I worked really hard, showed respect to colleagues, and formed a small team among staff members, which resulted in gaining the respect and the applause of the CMO (Marketing Head) of Ford. I was untouchable despite their silent groaning.

I worked there for a while and decided to head to another unit. I did it to give myself rest from the quenching fiery darts targeted at me. It made me cool off a little on the fact that Kraft and De Beers had been my star clients. I was tasked with international creative coordination and slept more on planes than in my Frankfurt flat. I was not the only one that knew how to turn the seas and it made me understand that everyone with an affluence must know how to turn the seas.

After some lunches, my head-hunter knew the right siren song to lure me to the Düsseldorf agency who was in dire need of a creative chairman, in Germany, Geschaeftsfuehrer. Working for the agency would attract benefits ranging from a better salary, a better car, a house allowance, and discretionary spending all included in the total package in store for me. Before I could start there, the agency was sold to another big agency with a hotshot CEO. The chaos I feared suddenly came to pass: my position was being questioned at the agency, but I had a three-year contract that lasted until I was 31.

I insisted and moved to Düsseldorf, Germany. I stayed in one of the 5-star hotels in the city and drove the company's Mercedes around. There was not much to do around there and one way to master the very thing that destroys happiness and hope is to avoid idleness and ill-talks.

So, I turned the sea again and started a mail order company with a colleague of mine. It was called Loving Fashion, which was about exquisite and sexy lingerie for ladies. I imagined selling the sexy catalog to make money on the catalog alone. I took that initiative, and I was happy that it worked out well. We made a lot of profit advertising alone, not even considering product sales.

After a year of back and forth, my contract paid off and I was 30 already, in a comfortable position that rewarded me for overcoming and the seas I have been turning. I had money, spare time, and an active mail order business. The success I felt was not in the hotel I was living in alone—it had already reached my former boss in Munich. He wanted me to come back to him, to work for him again. He made a significant offer that

I might have smiled at and accepted a few months ago with the star salary and the generous package associated with it.

*I blocked my ears and shunned the whistling wind from carrying the dusty words into my ears. I declined the offer with simplicity and with five words in my head: "**Never to be employed again.**"*

The mail order business was booming speedily. 100 people sent me 20 Deutsch Mark in an envelope to order a catalogue daily; I started some freelance gigs and placed a big PR story in the leading German ad magazine, which was why the money flowed in from the mail order business.

Spot the sea you want to turn and be logical in learning the best time to turn it. Mistakes will happen. You will gain your style from those mistakes. Stones might be hurled at you, but hold your shield in your hand, develop thick skin, and walk past the ones hurling the stones at you. Do it for yourself. Do it for your sanity.

One Moment Can Change it All

What breaks your heart could later set you on the right track. At times, one insult is enough to make you get yourself broken. One heartbreak from a person you loved too deeply could make your world fall apart or could mend your already broken world. It takes a day of happiness to forget all those excruciating memories or moments of our lives.

You cannot force someone else to like you because your abilities end in your vessel; your vessel is your territory and government. Your voice and actions can put an end to your governance if you give control to a foreign entity. It is never enough to start with something and end up being chased away by your own shadow. That is not a valid reason to stop yourself from moving into your realm of self-actualization, where you can be anything you want to be.

A simple math test can shed light on many people's state of mind. You remember going to school as a teenager. You sat for some compelling reason to pass your math test, for example. You made a lot of calculations just to get a specific figure after a few minutes of trying to get the result. Some other students finished earlier, while some finished after you. The first to finish the test does not necessarily mean that they will fail or pass. Some will get tired of sitting, looking for answers, and will resort to searching for the answers on someone else's sheet. Others might not know the answers to the calculations, but they still sit on their seats arrogantly, writing whatever they feel and submitting.

Mastering the chaos means training your mind

This is the actual case of chaotic history in our lineages. Some lineages are blocked because of the mindset that is not supposed to be static.

1. **The static-minded people** are the ones that many call *policy police*. They should have given room for a change. They birth more like them and remain static and unimaginative. The world is moving but our mindset is stuck in the past.

You cannot move into the present to gain access to the future. Everyone here will not move past each other; they will continue to wear the same shoes even though the sizes of their feet are different. They are full of traditions.

They never have new things.

2. **The *by-any-means-possible* people are never ready for the long process that a normal lifestyle entails. They want the fast life. They do not have the result of the calculations or problems they are faced with. They never wanted to study the flow of it to decipher their existence. They are impatient and easily irritated. They are always trying to do the things they saw others do what were evidently successful for them, and when it doesn't work the way they wanted it to, they bleed internally. These are the desperate ones. They end up as small- or big-time criminals based on the level of their greed. They are always ready to put their burdens on you; if you try to move, they will do everything they can to pull you back.**

3. **There is another category of people that I call *sapiens*.** They are not looking for anything to take away from you and would rather give you freely. The world loves the sapiens for their wisdom and discernment. They are masters of their emotions. They have everything planned out before going into it. They are mostly writers and scientists. Entrepreneurs find them good enough to invest in. We all know that entrepreneurs are never spending without thinking of the benefits (profit) in it for them. They are not selfish, greedy, or devilish. They are the

maintainers of the flow. The entrepreneurs help the economy flow and most of the entrepreneurs are always looking for economists. These people pump money into the economy for returns.

4. **The next category is the *silverbacks*.** These are the set of people that have someone to do everything for them and they are wired to never think otherwise. They have it all. They do not need to struggle with or for anything. They have the one moment most people crave for as their everyday lifestyle. They are always bored if they stay too long in one place. They are not ready to help you either unless they find it highly necessary.

5. **Another category is the *first-to-do*.** They are always trying to prove their strength, intelligence, importance, and so on. They are the critics of the world. They can bring your castle down. They are never the best option when it comes to searching for mentors. They find it hard to keep their attitudes internal, and will always show attitude to your face if you are lesser than your peers. They never correct out of love, but rather out of dislike and arrogance.

These are the people that you will be seeing a lot of as you try to embrace the chaos and move on with your life (mastering your emotions). Those categories can influence each other in a good or bad way. Be mindful of that and choose the category you want to fall in as well.

Many others tried to climb the ladder, but the wrong connections and associations cornered and shot their dreams in cold blood. You do not want to take the wrong step. Take your time and apply everything you have been learning about your situation.

I suffered a lot while growing up; it was World War III for me.

I knew what other members of my family did not take time to know.

Many live many years for one moment, but they get another one instead.

Martin Luther King Jr. was exposed to a different kind of unrest. He lived many years for one moment: to be an activist. The unrest gave him the chance to see his one moment and he got famous for it.

The founding father of Greek philosophy, Socrates, said, "Voting in an election is a skill, not a random intuition, and like every skill, it must be taught systematically to people. Letting citizen vote without an education is as irresponsible as putting them in charge of a trireme sailing to Samos in a storm."

Many great men and women that lived and are still living, learned from what everyone else is running from, and mastered how to bend it to bring out their ingenuity.

I lived many years for a moment—the kind of moment that could give my life a chance to be found in the world of success despite the unrest I felt while growing up. The unrest is what it took me to realize the one moment I needed to work towards. You can only discover the real one moment through unrest.

Do not run from the unrest. Go closer. Sit. Study. See the loopholes in the unrest to tame it. Running away from it cannot solve it; facing it like a diligent and courageous person will make you approach the unrest in a calculative manner.

Putting myself in a for success

It was all amplified after the big PR story in the German ad magazine. A marketing guy who founded an agency in Munich knew that I was based in Munich and asked me to be his partner with a 50/50 business partnership proposal.

Without much enthusiasm, I agreed. We started the business as partners. I deemed it slow at first because I had other plans and businesses, and he did not bring in any deals. After a couple of months I felt sorry for him because he was also the breadwinner for a family of 4 and with his meager salary he struggled a lot.

I knew that I was more skilled in turning the seas.

So I got more involved and rolled deals in with my ad portfolio. Things started moving fast at the agency. We moved out from the denouncing office we were using to an entire floor in central Munichs best location as things were going well. At this time, I also received a call from Werbeakademie München to be a lecturer and teacher, specifically teaching students about art and copywriting. Alongside this, I had a lot of international creative director freelance work, which made for very little free time.

We hired 30 employees to ensure the smoothest service was provided. Three years passed and my partner took the bait, thinking that he had learned enough to turn the seas. He felt the 50/50 partnership was expensive. He could not do it anymore. He preferred to start his own agency. He felt like he was competent to handle things.

I paid him out. I figured things out and kept the clients, which was contrary to what he thought would happen. I felt sorry for him and his career that ended shortly after our separation.

I was 35 at this point and everything at the agency was quickly expanding. I had foreseen myself going into another business that no one had started. I finally did it when I started working with Apple Computers. I imported them directly from the United States of America. The business grew and I grew as well.

I went into product placement in movies. I founded a media marketing agency; it was one of the first professional agencies to place products in movies, television shows, and cinemas. I had to work with various movie companies. Things ended when I discovered that the movie companies did not want to stick to the contract, so, I quit and turned to medical marketing in Munich. I hired more professionals to run the business. I bought a company named TRIMEX in Zug, Switzerland.

I moved to making business deals with big companies like CIBA, GEIGY, and ROCHE. We had an active contract and license (CIBA and GEIGY) to import and sell millions of ice packs to them. I have been blessed to be making a significant amount of money and my advertising agency expanded to Vienna. Together, with my new partner, I founded a branch in Los Angeles, USA.

I believe that nothing is wrong with our lives, it is only dynamic. The flow of the energies in a vessel manifests at a different pace. The real one moment is the purpose obtained from the many years lived for just a moment of success.

The script of your life can change

The story of the one moment for me cannot be complete without me telling you about my fall when debts from loans came upon me like a tsunami.

I was in a crashing moment, which I never wanted. Initially, only my monthly private fix-payments exceeded $50,000 (1990!). My agencies needed more than 1 Million a month. In today's money, this is perhaps double or triple.

Never ever I estimated that this will be a problem and I was quite sure to pay all debts off in a short period of time.

In just nine months, everything I had built fell apart. Contracts were cancelled. Management were fired. And some of the companies that I worked with were merged with another while some were sold. The bank was constantly calling my phone. I tried to think of a way out, but I could not find one. I shut down operations and closed the office in Vienna. The temporary solution I had was to reduce my staff by 80% and rent out half of my office space to another agency. Everything I had and stood for was at risk of damnation. This was great chaos for me.

I needed cash badly.

I invested in another business with a partner and named it Champagner Treff. It was a one-of-a-kind construction project on four wheels with television, entertainment, a bar, refreshments, and more.

A driver was hired to operate the truck with a wagon and placed it in Hamburg and other venues.

Slowly, the ad business started again on a low level. But we needed more cash. This pushed me into founding a company named ProTrade with a partner. We had the vision to sell traffic generators in drug stores. We won a big drugstore chain in Germany for this concept.

From the onset of it, business was great, but it turned out to be a horror movie when I got to know that my partner signed an additional contract stating that all unsold products could be sent back to us.

I had contact with some newly established private television companies and pitched the idea that they needed an attractive promotion. I convinced them to agree on an pay-per-order deal. In 24 hours, our television spots were in place and we had to take the travel orders. The deal was simply to fill empty hotels in Europe in low season, while the guests pay for food and drinks only. The business was nice, cash flow was good, but trouble came into the picture causing us to pull out, pay back money, and face legal issues. We closed the business and shut down the company. I was the first to sell empty beds with tele-shopping in Germany. However, perhaps I started this too early and without much knowledge of the organizational aspects of the business. The silver lining, though, was that TUI, the biggest player in travel business, asked me to come on board for consultations. It paid off somehow in the end.

I moved back to Austria and managed to win new clients— the most celebrated Austrian companies. I founded an agency in my house in Kirchberg and rented out my villa in Munich. I also moved into fancier and bigger offices in Munich.

It still wonders me how I could afford private schools in England and a private international university education for my kids.

My investment in education was perhaps to compensate for my own broken school career. I wanted to sell the villa for a reasonable price, but real estate was down.

First we rented it out and after some bad experiences we used it as a second home and the company headquarter.

The villa was sold in 2007 for the price I was always dreaming of.

When I was 57, I could afford to retire in wellness. I founded something else again, Brand Architect, besides my advertising agency on brand consulting.

I approached 60, and felt it was a good time to say thank you and farewell to the advertising world. I successfully sold the business and concentrated on brand architecture.

I also developed a new hobby called Trendguide Media. It was my first attempt at investing in multimedia, apps, and the likes;

everyone wanted to be a Trendguide partner. However, with the multimedia strategy, I was too early in the local markets. Most partners thought it was a money machine. Today, it is still running smoothly with the help of an Assistant, a few freelancers, and some very established self-employed partners and franchise owners.

The pandemic offered another chance to change paths and grow. I had to teach my first yoga lesson online. I moved on to take courses to become a certified meditation teacher because I loved my first experience. Furthermore, I partook in intense online and offline classes from the celebrity star, HypnoseMaster, and bestselling author, Gabriel Palacios in Switzerland. That has made me a certified HypnoseMaster, meditation teacher, and yoga teacher.

I am still a coach, adviser, and creative head for government officials, big companies, and celebrities, besides being a business angel with my investment company, Trendguide Capital.

Now I want to give back, share my experiences and the things I've learned on my journey, and encourage my readers to live up to their full potential and their dreams.

I was lucky and faced a lot of failures. I strived and never stopped learning to progress.

Part Four

LEADING THROUGH CHANGE

Navigating chaotic change can feel like trying to swim against the tide, with the world around you pushing you down with every inch you move forward. But you must keep your compass steady, and your gaze fixed on the horizon. It's important to remember that you are not alone and that you have the strength to weather the tornado coming your way. Even during chaos and uncertainty, you can find moments of calm and clarity. Change is a natural part of life and that it can also bring about new opportunities and growth. So, when the world around you pushes you down, remember to stay true to yourself, to keep moving forward, and to have faith that the sun will shine again.

Feeling Stuck

So far, we've discussed what to do in the face of change, but we haven't yet discussed how to bring about change when you are desperately searching for it. What if you're stuck and you can't find a way to move forward? How do you get yourself out of a situation that seems to be pulling you down, or out of an environment that is not conducive to your bright future?

Feeling stuck can be a frustrating and overwhelming experience, especially when you can't figure out how to change your life or your circumstances and you desperately want to. It can be easy to feel like you are at a dead end, with no way out and no clear path forward. And when this happens, the easy route is to just stay where you are. To give up and hope that something will change your circumstances—that a wind will come along and propel you forward. But that is hardly ever the case. Regardless, it is important to remember that this feeling is temporary and that there are ways to move past it.

To get unstuck and bring about change, you must first put in the work to identify the problem. This may require some self-reflection. Try to determine what is causing you to feel stuck. Is it a specific situation or circumstance, or is it a general feeling of dissatisfaction with your life? Once you have determined what the problem is, you can start producing with a plan that will help you address and resolve it.

Note that the change we are trying to bring about in these circumstances may be chaotic. It may require negative change to achieve your desired result. Let's look at an example to help us further illustrate this point.

Alex is a 45-year-old accountant who feels stuck in his company. He's been up for a promotion on several occasions, but for some reason, it always goes to someone else—even employees who've been at the firm for less time than he has. Confused and irritated, Alex feels as though he has remained stagnant for years, doing the same thing every day in the same position with the same people. He begins by identifying the problem, and realizes that to change his circumstances, he must quit his job. However, doing so is going to bring about immense change, as he will be forced to enter a competitive job market, which will be unfamiliar territory for him. He will be without pay for some time, will have to navigate life through an entirely different lens, and will have to face the chaotic change head-on. Although this step is necessary for his ultimate goal of moving forward, the change that it will bring about will be hard to navigate, regardless.

The next step in bringing about change is to set specific and achievable goals. Setting small, achievable goals can provide you with a sense of direction and purpose. These goals should be specific, measurable, and attainable (follow the SMART goal model for the most effective goal). For example, if you are feeling stuck in your career, you could aim to research different job opportunities or network with people in your industry. If you are feeling stuck in your personal life, you could set a goal of making new friends or trying out new activities you otherwise wouldn't have engaged in. It's also important to take action towards achieving your goals. Sometimes, when we feel stuck, we tend to get caught in a cycle of thinking and planning, without taking any actual steps to move forward. It's crucial to remind yourself that change won't happen overnight, and that it requires consistent effort and action.

Another helpful tip is to seek the support and guidance of others. Talking to a trusted friend or family member, or seeking out a therapist or counselor, can provide you with a new perspective and help you produce a plan of action that can help you achieve your goals and move forward. You can also join support groups, where you can connect with people who are going through similar experiences and learn from their perspectives.

With determination and the right mindset, you have the power to break free from the patterns that are holding you back and create the life you truly desire. Believe in yourself and your abilities, and have the courage to take the first step towards the change you want to see. Remember that the road ahead may be long and bumpy, but the journey will be worth it, and the reward will be a life full of fulfillment and purpose.

Feeling Like the World is Against You

It can be overwhelming to feel like the world is against you and that you are facing a lot of changes all at once. It can be a difficult and challenging time. Many people have gone through similar experiences and come out on the other side.

When you feel like the world is against you, it can be easy to become consumed by negative thoughts and feelings. You may feel like giving up or you may have convinced yourself that there is no hope. But it is important to remember that these thoughts and feelings are temporary and that you can surely overcome them if you put your mind to it.

Feeling like the world is against you can be both difficult and isolating. It can make you feel like you are alone and convince you that no one understands what you are going through. It can be hard to shake the feeling that everything is working and plotting against you, and that you are constantly being thwarted by invisible forces. But it's important to remember that you are not alone and that there are ways to cope with these feelings.

One of the best things to do when you feel like the world is against you is to identify the source of these feelings. Is it a specific event or situation that is causing them, or is it a general feeling of hopelessness and helplessness? Understanding the root cause of your feelings can help you better address them.

When the Change Has Already Consumed You

We discussed the effects negative change can have on the body, primarily manifesting as physical and mental symptoms felt throughout the body and mind. These effects, when left untreated, can fester and spread, making it even more difficult to rid yourself of them, change your perspective, and embrace change, acknowledging that it is entirely out of your control, and that your time and energy is better spent working toward your future and the things that *are* in your control.

If this is the position you've found yourself in, then you must reel yourself back in and force yourself back on track. This may mean employing the strategies we discussed above, including seeing a therapist, connecting with a support group, practicing meditation and mindfulness techniques, or writing in a journal. It is important that you identify that there is an issue first, address it by creating a specific plan that will allow you to overcome the hurdle, and develop skills that will ensure you are ready to face challenges next time, without allowing them to consume you.

We've already confirmed the fact that change is inevitable; so, surely, with a few extra tools in your toolkit, you'll be able to face changes when they're thrown at you without losing pieces of yourself, losing sight of your goals, or feeling consistent hopelessness and helplessness.

Setting Realistic Expectations

So far, this book has aimed to motivate you and help you come to terms with the fact that we can't change change. We can simply accept it when it comes our way, change it during the rare times that it's in our control, and focus on ourselves when we are in the midst of difficult and chaotic change.

However, it is imperative that we also discuss the importance of setting realistic expectations for ourselves, especially when we are facing negative change that can possibly spiral into more negative changes, more chaos, and therefore, more turmoil in our lives.

Setting realistic expectations is crucial when facing change, as it can prevent disappointment and help us more effectively manage our emotions. In this case study, we dive into the story of Jane, a young woman who recently lost her job and is now facing the challenge of finding a new one.

Jane had been working at her previous job for several years and had grown comfortable in her role. However, due to the current economic climate, her company was forced to downsize and unfortunately, Jane was one of the employees who lost their job. Initially, she felt a sense of shock and disappointment. She was unsure of what the future held and felt a sense of hopelessness as she tried to navigate new waters.

After some time spent dwelling on the situation, Jane decided to start actively searching for a new job. She began by setting small, achievable goals for herself. She made a list of companies she was interested in and set aimed to first update her resume, then apply to at least one new job each day. She also made a goal to attend at least one networking event each week that related to her field.

However, Jane tended to get her hopes up when she came across job opportunities that appeared to be the perfect fit. She would get excited about the possibilities and imagine herself in the role before even attending her first interview.

And so, what happened was that when she didn't get the job, she was left feeling hopeless and disheartened. She realized that her unrealistic expectations had set her up for disappointment and failure, and that she needed to adjust her mindset if she wanted to survive the changes she was experiencing, as she started feeling demotivated and no longer wanted to work toward her goals.

And so, Jane revised her goals and worked on setting more realistic expectations for herself. Instead of getting her hopes up, she wearily approached each one with a more balanced perspective. She reminded herself that finding a new job would take time given the current job market, and that it was okay if things didn't work out right away. She also made a point to focus on the small victories along the way, such as successfully completing an application or having a positive conversation with a potential employer. She started to see her self-worth in this process.

By setting more realistic expectations, Jane was able to more effectively manage her emotions. She didn't get as disappointed when things didn't work out and was able to keep herself motivated so she could continue her search for a new job. Eventually, she was hired at a new company in a role that seemed like a good fit for her, finally allowing her to start a new chapter in her life.

When change comes knocking, we have to set realistic expectations. By setting achievable goals, we can steadily navigate the violent waters of change, avoiding the rocky shores where failure, disappointment, and low self-esteem live. With a realistic outlook, we can face change head on, and emerge winners. Jane's story highlights the importance of not getting our hopes up and instead approaching situations with a more balanced perspective. By setting small, achievable goals and focusing on the small victories along the way, we can navigate change more effectively and find a path that works for us.

Change in the Workplace: Managing Resistance

Managing resistance to change is an important aspect of leading and implementing change in organizations and individuals. Resistance to change can come in various sources, such as employees, clients, or internally, and can manifest in many forms, including skepticism, fear, and apathy. Understanding and managing resistance to change is crucial for the successful implementation of change and achieving the desired goals and outcomes.

One way to manage resistance to change is to first understand and address the reasons behind it. People may resist change for a variety of reasons, like fear of the unknown, lack of trust in leadership, or feeling that the change will negatively impact their job or personal life. By understanding the root causes of resistance, leaders can directly address and resolve them and out to rest any fears that may have developed.

Another important aspect of managing resistance to change is communication. Clear, consistent, and transparent communication is essential in addressing concerns. It is important to involve stakeholders in the change process, by soliciting feedback and addressing concerns. Involving stakeholders in the process helps them feel more invested and less resistant, as we discussed in earlier sections.

Involving employees in the change also provides an opportunity for leaders to gain a better understanding of the potential challenges and opportunities associated with the change from a different perspective. By involving employees, leaders can also identify and address any potential roadblocks that may arise during the implementation process that they may have overlooked, since leaders tend to look at the bigger picture, while employees will look at the immediate effects, instead.

Another way to manage resistance to change is to provide training and support. Change can be difficult, and people may need extra guidance to adjust to new processes, procedures, or technologies. Providing training and support can help alleviate fears and concerns, while also increasing confidence in the change and its outcomes.

Leaders can also manage resistance to change by being flexible and open to feedback. Change can be difficult, and it's important to be open to feedback and willing to adjust the plan as needed. Being flexible and open to feedback can help build trust and buy-in from stakeholders, and ultimately increase the chances of successful change implementation.

Managing resistance to change also involves addressing the emotional side of change. Change can be difficult and stressful, and it's important to be aware of the emotional impact it can have on people. It's important to be compassionate and understanding, and to provide support for people who may be struggling with the change.

Establishing and Encouraging a Culture of Change

Creating a culture of change is crucial for organizations that want to be competitive and adapt to the everchanging business landscape. A culture of change refers to the overall attitude and mindset within an organization towards embracing and implementing change. It is characterized by a willingness to adapt, try new things, and continuously improve. A culture of change is one where individuals and teams are comfortable with—and even embrace—change as a requirement for properly and appropriately doing business. It is a culture that supports innovation, adaptability, and continuous improvement.

One key aspect of creating a culture of change is having a clear vision and strategy for change. This includes setting clear goals, outlining the steps to achieve them, and communicating them effectively to all stakeholders. Having a clear vision and strategy for change helps ensure that everyone is working towards the same goals and that the change is aligned with the overall mission, vision, and values of the organization.

Leadership also plays a crucial role in creating a culture of change. Leaders must guide by example and be willing to embrace change themselves. Moreover, they should be transparent and authentic in their communication, creating an open and inclusive environment in which employees feel comfortable sharing their thoughts and ideas, and feel as though they will not be judged.

According to a study conducted by KPMG, organizations with a culture of change are five times more likely to be successful in their digital transformation efforts.[8] This is because a culture of change allows organizations to quickly and effectively respond to new technologies, changes in technological advancement, and market trends. Additionally, organizations with a culture of change are more likely to have employees who are engaged and motivated, which leads to higher levels of productivity and job satisfaction.[9]

Creating a culture of change involves having a clear vision and strategy for change, involving employees in the change process, strong leadership, providing ongoing training and support, recognizing and rewarding employees, and being flexible and open to feedback. By creating a culture of change, organizations can increase the chances of successful change implementation and achieve desired outcomes.

The Role of Leaders

Leadership plays a crucial role in navigating change in the workplace. The type of leader that is best equipped to lead during times of change is one that can effectively communicate, collaborate, and build trust and rapport with team members. According to a study by McKinsey & Company, 75% of change initiatives fail to achieve their goals, and one of the main reasons for this is a lack of effective and appropriate leadership.[10] To

8 KPMG. (2018). Culture for a digital age. Retrieved from https://home.kpmg/content/dam/kpmg/pdf/2018/09/culture-for-a-digital-age.pdf
9 Kotter, J. P. (1996). Leading change. Harvard Business Press.
10 Kotter, J. P. (1996). Leading change. Harvard Business Press.

effectively lead during change, it is crucial for leaders to hone in a combination of specific skills and characteristics related to navigating change.

One of the best types of leaders during change is a transformational leader. These leaders inspire and motivate their employees to not only accept change but to also assume responsibility to drive the change forward.[11] They create a sense of shared vision and purpose, and empower their employees to become leaders themselves within their team and department. This breeds a culture in which employees are more likely to embrace and support the change initiative, rather than rebel against is, thus resulting in genuine buy-in, which is good for the business overall. Transformational leaders also have the ability to create a sense of community and belonging within their team, which is especially important during times of change.

Another important aspect of leadership during change is emotional intelligence (EI). Leaders with high EI are able to effectively manage their emotions and the emotions of others, which is crucial during times of change.[12] They are able to empathize with their employees and understand the impact of change on them. This helps to build trust and improves communication and collaboration during the change process. Additionally, leaders with high EI are able to create a positive work environment, which can help to reduce resistance to change.

---

11 Bass, B. M. (1990). Bass & Stogdill's handbook of leadership: Theory, research, and managerial applications (3rd ed.). Free Press.
12 Goleman, D. (1998). What makes a leader?. Harvard Business Review, 76(6), 93-102.

Leaders who are also good at strategic thinking are also crucial during change. They are able to identify and analyze potential opportunities and challenges, and develop a plan to navigate them.[13] This is important for leaders during change as it enables them to anticipate potential roadblocks and pro-actively address them. Additionally, strategic thinking leaders are able to align the change initiative with the overall goals and objectives of the organization, which helps to ensure its success.

Covid-19 as the Catalyst of Change

The Covid-19 pandemic has brought about unprecedented changes in terms of both our personal and professional lives. The sudden shift to remote work, social distancing, and numerous lockdowns worldwide has forced individuals and organizations to adapt to new ways of living and working.

In terms of personal changes, the pandemic has resulted in increased stress and anxiety levels for many individuals. A survey conducted by the American Psychological Association found that 63% of adults reported that their mental health has been negatively impacted due to the pandemic.[14] Additionally, the pandemic has led to changes in daily routines, social isolation, and financial insecurity, as many have been laid

---

13 Ireland, R. D., & Hitt, M. A. (1999). Achieving and maintaining strategic competitiveness in the 21st century: the role of strategic leadership. Academy of management executive, 13(1), 43-57.

14 American Psychological Association. (2020). Stress in America: Coping with Change. Retrieved from https://www.apa.org/research/action/speaking-of-psychology/coping-change

off or forced to work less hours due to changing lockdown regulations.

In the professional realm, the pandemic has accelerated the shift towards remote work. Prior to the pandemic, only a few companies offered permanent remote work, or even a hybrid model. However, a survey conducted by Gartner found that 41% of employees plan to permanently shift to remote work post-pandemic.[15] This shift has led to changes in communication and collaboration methods, as well as the need for new technologies and infrastructure to support remote work.

The pandemic has also resulted in changes in consumer behavior and business operations. A survey conducted by McKinsey found that consumer behavior has shifted towards online shopping and contactless payment.[16] This has led to an increase in e-commerce and a shift towards digital marketing. Additionally, many businesses have had to adapt to new safety protocols and find ways to continue operations while facing supply chain disruptions and decreased demand.

---

15 Gartner. (2020). Gartner HR Survey Reveals 41% of Employees Likely to Work Remotely at Least Some of the Time Post Coronavirus Pandemic. Retrieved from https://www.gartner.com/en/newsroom/press-releases/2020-04-14-gartner-hr-survey-reveals-41--of-employees-likely-to-

16 Kohil, S. (2020). How COVID-19 is changing consumer behavior—now and forever. Retrieved from https://www.mckinsey.com/~/media/mckinsey/industries/retail/our%20insights/how%20covid%2019%20is%20changing%20consumer%20behavior%20now%20and%20forever/how-covid-19-is-changing-consumer-behaviornow-and-forever.pdf

Leading Through Changes
Brought on by Covid-19

The Covid-19 pandemic has served as a powerful lesson for leaders and individuals alike regarding the importance of adaptability and the ability to navigate change suddenly and without a plan. Leaders were forced to quickly pivot and make difficult decisions in order to keep their organizations and employees safe and operational, while also ensuring that they were adhering to changing rules and regulations, such as testing requirements.

One of the most significant changes brought about by the pandemic has been the need for effective crisis management. Crisis management is the process of preparing for, responding to, and recovering from a crisis. It is a critical skill that is essential for both organizations and individuals in times of uncertainty and change. Leaders have had to make difficult decisions and navigate rapidly changing circumstances in order to keep their organizations afloat. They have had to be agile and responsive in order to respond to the pandemic's impact on their employees, customers, and operations. Additionally, many leaders have had to navigate the financial impact of the pandemic on their organizations and find ways to sustain their operations.

Now that Covid-19's effects on society and the workforce have subsided to some degree, it's crucial to consider the other troubles looming that will most certainly test leadership. For instance, we have to consider inflation, the war in Ukraine, coping with permanent effects of an escalation, and so on. This indicates to us that our environment is everchanging, and although Covid-19 has started to fade into the background, there are other issues—just as significant—threatening to test us once more, and will likely accompany us in coming years.

Where We're Headed

Our world is changing every so rapidly, making it crucial for us to adapt in the face of change that is both expected and unexpected. With technology rising at a speed we have never witnessed before, and our times changing by the day, we must learn to embrace change in a way that does not allow us to lose ourselves or our way. We must embrace change in a way that allows us to propel forward, leaving the past behind us and focusing on the future we still have ahead.

Although this is all much easier said than done, we must consider the techniques provided above to help us through said changes. There's no predicting what tomorrow has in store for us. And with this in mind, we can either dwell on the stress and anxiety of the unknown or the unfamiliar, or we can choose to adapt to an everchanging society in which the unexpected and the uncertain will forever be out of our control. Why allow our lives to be dictated by that we cannot control? Instead, we must take hold of our emotions, feelings, and actions, all of which we *can* control and *can* change.

With a mindset like this, we will be prepared for any type of change, whether personal, professional, or a mixture of the two. We will be prepared for a job loss, financial strain, a restructuring, a family issue, and more. We will be prepared to face it all when we choose to focus on only that which we can control.

The rest, we must leave up to the universe.

CONCLUSION

My story is meant to motivate you, not to disconnect you from the dream that you have always imagined because of some bad news or bad moments.

Everything about a person is a story for another man to tell for a long time. The stories are either inspiring for the other man to get a hold of himself or to encourage his bad attitude or incorrect ideas. You are living in this world, and you are not sick. You are full of strength and passion. The relationship that is not working does not determine your personality. Your colleagues and bosses at work are the limit to your drive and the bridge you have to pass through to reach your goal.

Not everyone will like you. Not everyone will hate you. Not everyone will want you at the top of your career while some don't give a damn about it. Many things can go wrong in your life but do not let everything about you sink because of the shattered glass on the floor.

My story of rise and fall, fall and rise made me start giving back through writing to assist people in ways that gears personal growth and development, to reassure you that a purposeful moment is coming at the end of the trial. I feel more at peace and fulfilled doing the things I am doing now. I am by no means perfect, but the journey has taught me so much that I'd simply like to impart.

With delight, I'll leave you with this: "Don't limit yourself because of the situation around you, push through it, rewrite your own story and let people have something peculiarly positive to talk about. You're the author of your story, write it!"

A Note from the Author

If you enjoyed this title and would like to read about other topics that have changed my life, please check out my new books on Amazon or my website: www.my-mindguide.com.

Also, let's stay connected on social media. Please drop a line on Facebook or Instagram and stay tuned for updates! You're welcome to share your thoughts with me directly as well through email: gassner@my-mindguide.com. In return, I'll send you a gorgeous infographic that you can cut out and frame.

Also, please leave a review on Amazon, as this will help me reach an even broader audience. Thank you so much for your time, insight, and undying hunger for knowledge!

On that note, I want to thank all my colleagues, clients, friends, and family members, who have all contributed to the person I have now become.

I also want to thank Gabriel Palacios, the king of hypnotherapy and a Swiss bestseller author who taught this old fox new tricks, letting me deep-dive into the mystery of hypnotherapy. I learned so much along the journey to the point where I'm now a certified master-hypnosis coach and conversation coach myself!

Furthermore, I want to say thank you to the fantastic teachers of SAMYANA/Bali who trained me to become a certified yoga and meditation teacher.

Last but not least, I want to give a special thanks to my master-teacher, Eckhard Wunderle, who's close to a saint to me. He introduced me to the world of meditation and let me discover all the wonders it has to offer. I couldn't be prouder for having received my certification as a meditation teacher directly from him at the Institut für Spirituelle Psychologie.

Peace, love, and happiness to all of you—until next time!

ABOUT THE AUTHOR

Kurt Friedrich Gassner is an Austrian self-improvement author who empowers his readers to better navigate the intricacies of the unconscious mind. Through his lived experience and extensive knowledge of cutting-edge psychology, he helps people actualize their fullest potential. What started as writing for his peers in exchange for drawings at the age of fourteen, and later working as a professional copywriter, ultimately turned into becoming the creative director of multiple international agencies and becoming the author of numerous self-help books.

However, writing isn't this entrepreneurial spirit's sole passion; Kurt has also been a serial founder and business angel, garnering four decades' worth of expertise in the global advertising and brand consulting sectors. As a result, he has earned numerous awards in the areas of creative directing, direct marketing, and training, and became a self-made millionaire. Utilizing his free time during the global lockdown, he even immersed himself in hypnotherapy and is now a licensed hypnotherapist, yoga instructor, and meditation teacher.

When he isn't running his businesses, consulting with leaders, or writing about the unconscious mind, you can find this globetrotter traveling around the world, golfing, biking in the

Alps, attending the opera, or hiking. He is also the proud father of two successful children.

Currently, he splits his time between Munich, Germany, and Kirchberg, Austria.

Throughout his life of innumerable toughs and crests, Kurt Friedrich Gassner has unyieldingly continued to live by the following motto: **"Never stop! The best is yet to come..."** And it is through his unwavering determination and perseverance that he has led a life of personal prosperity, learning countless invaluable lessons along the way. To him, a life lived without sharing one's acquired wisdom isn't a fulfilling one, so he creates books as a way of giving back and making this world a better place than when he first entered it. Some of his publications include *The Power of Forgiveness*, , *Soul-Match, Can You Inherit a Poisoned Mind?*, and *The Bliss of Struggle*. When he was thirty, he wrote a best-selling children's book that sold over one million copies and was used in kindergarten classrooms in German-speaking countries.. Visit Kurt's official website to unleash your inner power and harness it for the greater good: www.my-mindguide.com

SELF-EMPOWERMENT BOOKS

SELF-EMPOWERMENT BOOKS

SELF-EMPOWERMENT BOOKS

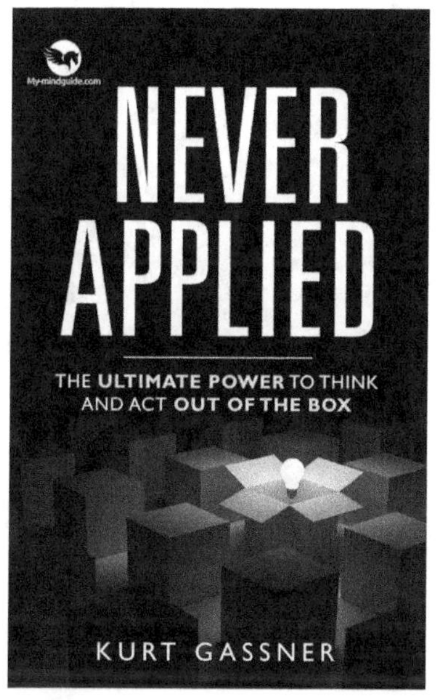

SELF-EMPOWERMENT BOOKS

SELF-EMPOWERMENT BOOKS

SELF-EMPOWERMENT BOOKS

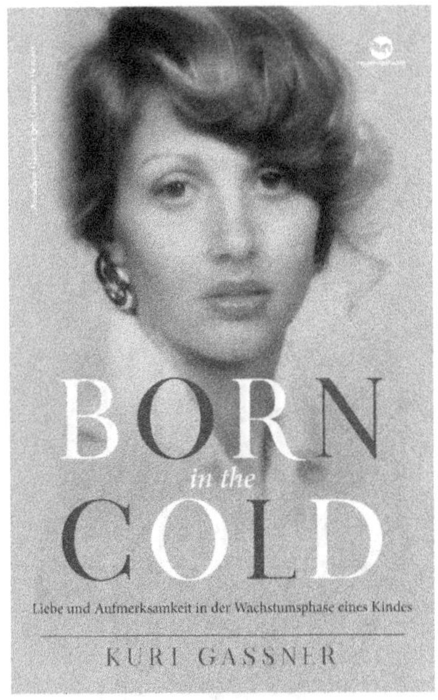

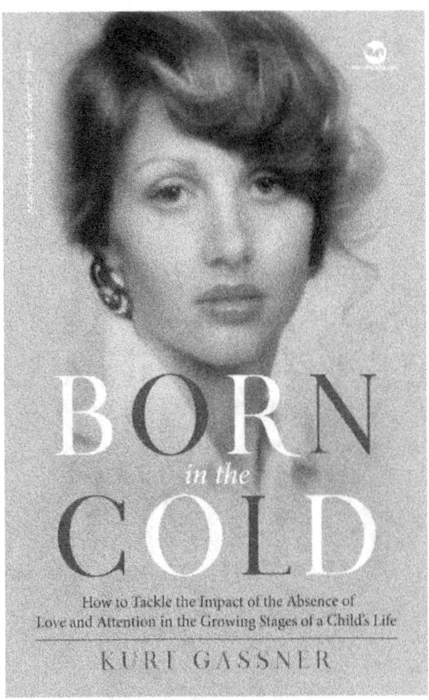

CHILDREN BOOKS

SELF-EMPOWERMENT BOOKS

SELF-EMPOWERMENT BOOKS

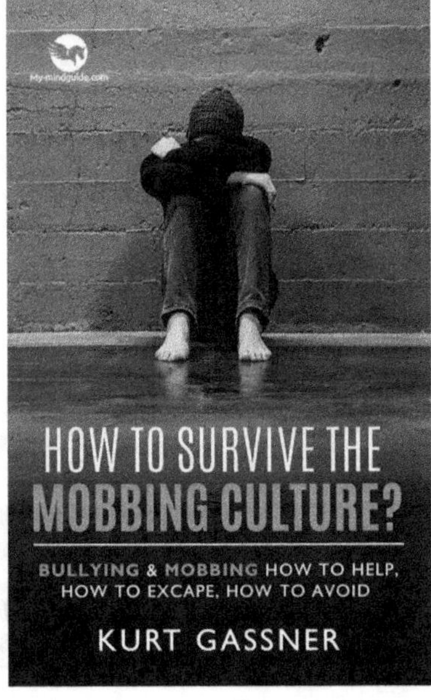

SELF-EMPOWERMENT BOOKS

MINDFUL BUSINESS BOOKS

MINDFUL BUSINESS BOOKS

MINDFUL BUSINESS BOOKS

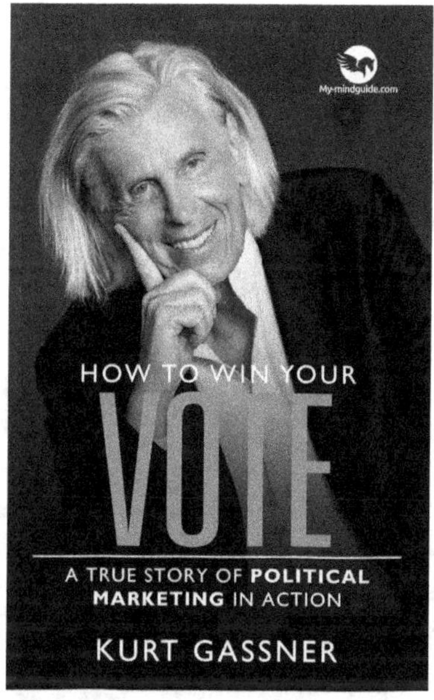

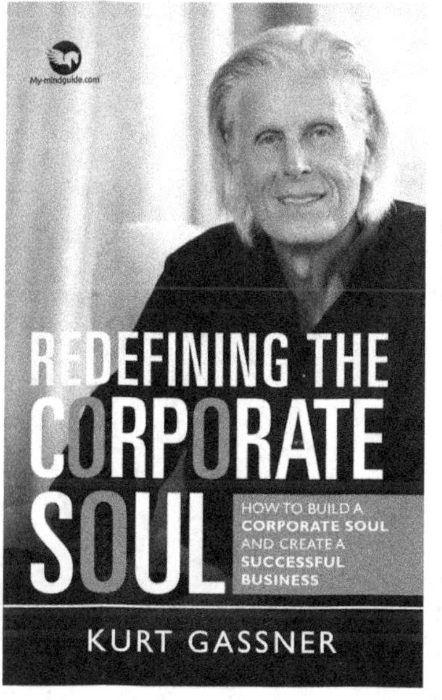

BESTSELLING AUTHOR OF
The Art Of
FORGIVNESS
AMAZON #1 BESTSELLER
My-mindguide.com
A practical guide for self healing and overcome past traumas
The Art Of
FORGIVNESS
KURT GASSNER
The Art Of
FORGIVNESS
KURT GASSNER

You Can reach Author's Wikipedia